CW00419135

LORD MASON

Outside 10 Downing Street, c.1975 (MA)

LORD MASON

Barnsley Pit Lad to Peer

A Life Illustrated

Brian Elliott

DEDICATION

For Marjorie

First published in Great Britain in 2008 by
Wharncliffe Books
an imprint of
Pen & Sword Books Ltd
47 Church Street
Barnsley
South Yorkshire
S70 2AS

ISBN 978 1 84563 036 2

A CIP catalogue record for this book is
available from the British Library

Printed and bound in Great Britain
By CPI UK

Pen & Sword Books Ltd incorporates the Imprints of
Pen & Sword Aviation, Pen & Sword Family History,
Pen & Sword Maritime, Pen & Sword Military, Wharncliffe Local History,
Pen & Sword Select, Pen & Sword Military Classics, Leo Cooper,
Remember When, Seaforth Publishing and Frontline Publishing

For a complete list of Pen & Sword titles please contact
PEN & SWORD BOOKS LIMITED
47 Church Street, Barnsley, South Yorkshire, S70 2AS, England
E-mail: enquiries@pen-and-sword.co.uk
Website: www.pen-and-sword.co.uk

Contents

Foreword

I feel privileged to be asked to write the Foreword of this book about the life of Lord Mason. Barnsley has produced many distinguished people, but unlike many, Lord Mason was elected and I believe this is important because he is the representative of the people. He is a great son of Barnsley.

Roy is one of the politicians I really admire. Coming from a humble background like myself – starting in the coal mines at the age of 14 – he worked his way through life with great effort and strength of character from 1953, when he was first elected to Parliament, to today.

His strength of character was recognised by Prime Minister James Callaghan, when he decided to make Roy the Secretary of State for Northern Ireland (1976 to 1979). This followed many other Ministerial and Secretary of State appointments.

He certainly made his mark in Northern Ireland. In an article in the *Daily Telegraph* of 18 April 2004 by Geoffrey Wheatcroft headed 'Happy 80th Birthday to the IRA's most deadly foe' Geoffrey Wheatcroft said: 'Even now Sinn Fein and the large penumbra of republican fellow-travellers in Ulster and Dublin spit at the mention of Mason's name. And for why? Quite simply because, as Martin McGuinness said, "Mason beat the shit out of us."' I often wonder if Labour had not lost the 1979 election, and Roy Mason had remained in office, whether the problems of Northern Ireland would have been solved much sooner.

I had a conversation with Harold Wilson in the late 1950s when as a young and very raw NUM Official I was attending my first conference away from home at Bingley College. Wilson, another young Yorkshire achiever, said to me, 'I hope the Yorkshire miners will send us some more Roy Masons.' As time passed and I recognised Roy's achievements I understood what Wilson meant. These achievements are far too many to record here, but I believe Roy has been the most outstanding Yorkshire MP the NUM ever produced.

Barnsley and the whole country should be proud and be grateful to a wonderful man who has never left his roots. I know he could never have achieved all that he has without the wonderful support of his wife, Lady Marjorie and their family. She has always been at his side and still is. My life has been enriched and my mind educated through my friendship with Roy and his family and I am sure, as the years go by, students of politics and public life will use this book and come to admire the achievements of this Barnsley boy.

The Lord Lofthouse of Pontefract
The House of Lords

Geoffrey Lofthouse

Preface

Brian Elliott was born in Royston, my birthplace too, and indeed taught at Royston Secondary school where I had attended some years before. As a regional historian of note he has built up a remarkable knowledge of my home town of Barnsley and its neighbourhood. His work has been especially detailed and much appreciated concerning its coalmining heritage and pit disasters, particularly the personal and human views of families of the dead and injured, research and writing of national importance.

His new book is based on my vast archive of printed sources and photographic material relating to my personal and political life, my many visits to foreign lands, meeting heads of state and world leaders, my life as a Barnsley MP and cabinet minister under Harold Wilson and James Callaghan; and my continuing campaigns and interests in the House of Lords. Brian and myself have spent countless hours together at my home, examining my portfolios of illustrative material. He has carried out a series of interviews with me and has visited me in Parliament, especially the House of Lords and was present at my recent conferment as an Honorary Freeman of the Metropolitan Borough of Barnsley. I am absolutely delighted that such a local author of distinction has compiled this historic and detailed picture of my life and times – and feel content that it will stand the examination of time.

Mason of Barnsley

At home, sorting material from the Mason Archive. (BEC)

Lord Mason with author Brian Elliott in 1999

Introduction and Acknowledgements

Compiling an honest biography of a living person is a very difficult task for any writer. Anyone who has tried to do so will appreciate my opening remark. The process is compounded through really getting to know an individual and to some extent his family and close contacts over time.

What I can also truthfully say is that I have been allowed total access to a vast range and quantity of material; and I have received a good number of contributions from former colleagues. Whenever I have requested information it has been provided, even during the difficult period of Lord Mason's recent illness. In addition, I have made use of a variety of contemporary and modern sources in order to supplement, clarify and better appreciate local and national events. A chronology relating to Mason's life and times whilst he was an MP will hopefully provide some context to each picture sequence.

A good number of relevant items were undated and needed a lot of research in order to place them in context. Inevitably, mistakes may have been made in this process, for which I apologize and welcome further clarification. Every effort has been made to attribute and acknowledge pictures, though again a vast number of unstamped photographs made this task extremely difficult.

Over the years, particularly after Mason became a senior politician, he attracted the interests of many talented cartoonists. Several, such as Rowell Friers, became friends, and many presented him with their original drawings. I am grateful to Lord Mason for allowing me access to his large collection of original cartoon artwork.

Although Mason never kept a diary in the style of Benn, Castle or Crossman, he did accumulate a vast collection of photographic images, documents and artifacts. These form the basis of this book which is essentially a pictorial appreciation of his life and times. However, a good number of items were undated and lacking in context, so a lot of time was spent in researching individual and groups of illustrations. Inevitably mistakes may have been made for which I apologize and clarification is welcome.

Even so, it would have been relatively easy to assemble a random collection of pictures but I have hopefully tried to do so in order to both respect and tell the story of someone who became a leading figure in the Labour Party and in twentieth century British politics.

The overview at the start of each part of the book is intended to set the scene for the accompanying illustrations. It is also based on a series of recorded interviews carried out by myself, alongside researched information and material from his autobiography, published in 1999. Undoubtedly the hardest sections to compile relate to the key and very demanding periods in Mason's life and career, most notably as Secretary of State for Northern Ireland and his embattled final years as a shadow minister and backbencher.

Many individuals and organisations have contributed to the book in various ways and I apologize for any omissions. My special thanks go to Lord and Lady Mason and the Mason family for their tremendous help and support. Without their co-operation this collection and assembly of images and words would not have been possible. Lord Lofthouse responded immediately to my request for him to write the Foreword, for which I am most grateful; and also for his kindness when I met him at the House of Lords and at his Pontefract home. The staff at the House of Lords Library responded to my requests (via Lord Mason) for information with great efficiency. In addition, I would like to thank the House of Lords and House of Commons for allowing me access to the building and for permission to take photographs (again via requests from Lord Mason). Those who provided wordage for the tribute section through either a direct request or via previously unpublished or published material, namely Dickie Bird, Tony Blair MP, Gordon Brown MP, PM, the late Lord Callaghan, Lady Falkender, Linda McAvan, Mel Dyke, Councillor Stephen Houghton, Lord Lofthouse, Lord Molyneaux, Councillor Mike Stokes and Lord Varley did so with great appreciation from Lord and Lady Mason and myself. As ever, my thanks to my publishers, in particular Charles Hewitt and his colleagues at Wharncliffe/Pen & Sword Books for their support, and indeed their patience; and to the Barnsley Chronicle whose coverage of local events is an indispensable source of information.

Most of the illustrations used in the book are from the Mason Archive (MA), loaned to me by Lord Mason and given to him for his use by a large number of photographers and organisations over many years. Some images are from Lord Mason's own camera or from my own camera or collection (BEC). The Mason Cartoon Archive (MCA), as already noted, consists of mainly original artwork, again presented to Lord Mason for his collection and usage by individual artists. A further large archive of material is lodged in Barnsley Archives and Local Studies. Both may merge in the near future. The Trustees of the Victorian Village Museum at Cawthorne kindly allowed me access to photograph artifacts and material in their Mason collection. Wherever possible I have also tried to gain permission for the use of copyright material and credits/ownership is given after each picture caption. Unfortunately, there were many unstamped images, where ownership has been impossible trace for which our apologies are unreservedly given. Stan Bulmer (Stan Plus Two Photographers) of Barnsley gave permission for the use of several modern images of Lord and Lady Mason and their family; and known images from the Barnsley Chronicle are credited.

Other contributing individuals and organisations for which I am grateful include Maureen Anderson, Barnsley Metropolitan Borough Council, Thelma Carnevale, Council of Europe Archive (Benjamin Palermiti), The College of Arms, Arthur Cummings (cartoonist), Daily Express, Daily Mail, Dentons & Co (Barnsley photographers), Doncaster Local Studies Library, Angela Elliott, National Railway Museum (York), Rowell Friers (cartoonist), The Guardian, The Guardian Digital Archive, Leslie Illingworth (cartoonist), Irish Times, News of the World, North-East Lincolnshire Library Service, Raymond Jackson (cartoonist), John Jenson (cartoonist), Howard Jones, Thelma McLoughlan, June Mendoza, John Musgrave-Wood (cartoonist), The Observer, Ordnance Survey, Mike Pattison, Registrar's Office

(Barnsley), Tom Richmond (Yorkshire Post), Roy Sabine (Barnsley photographer), Scout Association, Chris & Pearl Sharp (Old Barnsley), Sheffield Morning Telegraph, The Sun, Sunday Telegraph, The Times, Arthur Wakefield, Glan Williams (cartoonist) and Elizabeth Wright (Mayor's Office, Barnsley MBC).

Tributes

It is an absolute privilege to count Roy - Lord Mason - as a friend who was such a staunch supporter during my career as a cricket umpire. Our careers may have been different - his in politics, mine in cricket - but we have done much to put Barnsley on the map. I will always be grateful for his kindness and friendship: it was a great honour to rush from Lord's, after umpiring in my 100th international, to the Houses of Parliament for a special dinner that dear Roy had organised in my honour. From Lord's to the Lords in one day, who would have thought it? But politics, and in particular his work in Northern Ireland, was only one aspect of Roy's varied and distinguished life - as this book testifies. I'm honoured to be just one small footnote in this long and distinguished story that is a huge credit to Roy, his family and his many friends.

Dickie Bird MBE

I very much enjoyed our recent meeting [June, 2007] when we talked about your extraordinary fifty-four years as an MP and Member of the House of Lords. It was especially fascinating to learn of the circumstances of your time as Secretary of State for Northern Ireland, and of the three Cabinet positions you occupied with such distinction. You have made a huge contribution to public life over so many years, and we are all immensely grateful to you.

Tony Blair MP, Prime Minister [June 2007]

Your career in the House of Commons spanned three decades. When you were first elected to Parliament I was only two years old, which just shows we are both getting on a bit! You are an inspiration, and your story is legendary: you left school at 14, went down the pit straight after, but nevertheless worked your way up to the Cabinet table at 10 Downing Street. Not only did you hold some of the highest offices in the land, but you were always highly regarded across the political spectrum, and this remains the case today. We in the Labour Party are proud of you, but even the *Daily Telegraph* calls you a hero. I wanted to add my thanks to all those who have gathered to honour you.

Rt Hon Gordon Brown MP, Prime Minister [November 2007]

I have just returned as a guest of the of the Advanced Command course, Joint Services Staff College at Shrivenham, near Swindon. If Roy could have been with me he wopuld have been much cheered! The Commodore who arranged and supervised that memorable briefing regarding the Sea Harrier that Roy received at the Dunford airfield in Surrey was also present. Just how fateful was that visit and Roy's subsequent stand and courage in the face of hostility was all too well borne out in the Falklands conflict. Men like the Commodore never stop singing Roy's praises!

Another guest, a retired Colonel, suddenly shouted at the large gathering: 'Roy Mason was the best Defence Secretary we ever had.' He is still held in great esteem.

Sir Patrick Duffy (in a letter to Lady Mason, July 2008).

When Barnsley's MP Roy Mason became The Right Honourable The Lord Mason of Barnsley in 1987 he took as his motto 'Courage and Integrity'. It was a sound choice since the words have come to typify his record of 55 years of unbroken service in the Houses of Parliament. As one of the country's youngest MPs, the new Member for Barnsley was given conflicting advice but took a conscious decision in 1953 to follow the words of wisdom of an older colleague: 'Look the part, be the part and always observe the niceties of the House in addressing it.' He has unerringly done that in manner which remains humorous and informed whilst unassumingly courteous – and a great deal more. An unflinching politician and a man of conviction who would fight tooth and nail for a cause or principle, he is a reliable friend whose advice is as sound as it is sensitive. Barnsley's name is in good hands.

Mel Dyke
Barnsley author and Educationalist [July 2008]

You have made a good start [on achieving 50 years in Parliament], and now I expect you to keep it up. I see every sign that your early promise will develop into full maturity if you go on as you are doing! But no slacking! And love to Marjorie who deserves the credit!

Lord Callaghan of Cardiff [April, 2003]

Roy Mason was regarded by Harold Wilson as a dependable and long-standing supporter of the Party over many years. Roy had the great advantage in having come from the Miners' Union, with whom he enjoyed a lifelong connection. His career in government reflects his remarkable flexibility and is testament to Harold's regard for him as he could do justice to every job to which he was a appointed. He and Harold were contemporaries in many senses. They both came to the Commons as young men, both were excellent communicators and their careers showed a likeness. Although they had differences of opinion, they never clashed. They both enjoyed pipe and cigar smoking. For my part, I took the view that Roy was a young and, to me, very personable member of the government. On a lighter note, Harold thought Roy had a distinction in designing ties, particularly for organisations that didn't have their own, which appealed to him.

Baroness Falkender (formerly Marcia Williams, Harold Wilson's Personal and Political Secretary). [May 2007]

Lord Mason has had a long, dedicated and splendid political career. He is the only Barnsley resident ever to achieve a position within the Cabinet Office and has taken on some of the most difficult positions in Government, not least of which being Secretary of State for Northern Ireland. However, whatever Roy did in the past as a Member of Parliament or in the House of Lords, he always worked hard for Barnsley and its people. He is Labour through and through and his values of loyalty, hard work and commitment are the values of all good politicians. We recently gave Roy the honorary title of Freedom of the Borough which was the least we could do for the work he has done, not only for the country but for Barnsley in particular.

Stephen Houghton CBE, Leader, Barnsley Metropolitan Council [Jan 2008]

The miners were indebted to him then and they have been indebted to him ever since. I am certain that no other miner has represented his area – the Barnsley coalfield – in Parliament for 50 years. As a former miner myself, I have great pleasure in paying tribute to him.

Lord Lofthouse of Pontefract [speaking in the House of Lords, April 2003]

Congratulations on your fifty years in Westminster, and your lifelong commitment to the Labour movement in South Yorkshire, hope you enjoy the thrill of political life for many more years.

Linda McAvan MEP (Yorkshire and Humber), Deputy Leader of the European Labour Party [April 2003]

Our last Secretary of State from the ranks of Labour was Roy Mason...and was probably the best we have had. He would not talk to terrorists or to any party with any obvious links to terrorists. Obviously he saw it as his task, first and foremost, to deflect terrorism and, only when terrorism was defeated, to decide on the way forward for this part of the United Kingdom. Naturally, he took advice from his security chiefs and from the Northern Ireland Office but he was always seen as the man in charge.

R Finlay McCance (Letter to Belfast Telegraph, July 1997)

Mason beat the shit out of us.

Martin McGuinness MP [quoted in the Guardian, Sept 1993]

The day he was appointed Secretary of State for Northern Ireland, Roy Mason flew to Stormont and on his return to London the following day he invited me to meet him...along with three civil servants...His first words were: 'Now what do you want?' I retorted: 'You invited me!' Roy's response was: 'Yes, but you know what you want, so tell me what is on your list.' Thus encouraged, I submitted my first request. The new Secretary of State, with little delay, said: 'Yes, I can do that.' My point number 7 was met with a put down: 'Forget it!' We followed on to my final point, 10, and when I got to my office I discovered that we had agreed on eight and a half points. Real business by both of us! That is how we worked with Roy.

Lord Molyneaux of Killead KBE (formerly Jim Molyneaux, Leader of the Ulster Unionists).

He is dapper and forever cheerful and totally belies his age. Even to this day many senior politicians, Labour and Conservatives alike, describe him as the best Ulster Secretary there ever was. And almost as proof of that is the fact that today, decades later, he still merits tight police security. His achievements are endless. He managed to winkle £70 million out of the Treasury to develop the Sea Harrier, an aircraft which served the nation so well in the Falklands conflict in 1982. He was also, he says, personally responsible for the highly successful National Exhibition Centre in Birmingham.

Chris Moncrieff ('Cobbett'), The House Magazine [April 2003]

The Labour shadow cabinet has nine Oxford graduates, most of them in the top jobs: and Roy Mason stands out as the solitary worker.

Anthony Sampson, The New Anatomy of Britain (pp60/661, 1971)

Roy never left Barnsley, he stayed with his roots. He made close contact with the Party and his voters – albeit this was a little restricted when he had a 'heavy' bodyguard but within those constraints we still toured towns, pubs and clubs on a very regular basis, often conducting a 'surgery' at the bar (not the legal one!). He was one of the very few working class lads to come off the coal face and reach some of the highest offices of the land – a remarkable success story. The decisions he made on Ireland, whilst very difficult for him (and his family), he did what he thought was right and I think his actions are vindicated by history. There is peace and a more just society in Northern Ireland today.

Barnsley MBC Councillor Mike Stokes (Mason's last political agent) [July 2008]

Roy Mason had a distinguished career as a Labour Cabinet Minister. As a man who left school at 14 and went to work underground in the pit his achievements are without parallel. As a fellow Cabinet Minister it was a joy and privilege to work alongside him. In Cabinet and Cabinet Committees he was always in command of his subject and earned the respect and admiration of his colleagues. When the general policies of the Government were under discussion his forthright contribution and common sense was always appreciate. Above all, he was loyal. Loyal to his fellow members of the Cabinet and to the doctrine of collective responsibility, an attribute not always possessed or observed by some of his colleagues. i know he was held in high esteem by both Harold Wilson and Jim Callaghan in whose Cabinets he served.

Baron Varley PC (of Chesterfield, formerly Eric Varley) [April 2007]

Roy Mason is one of the unsung heroes of the Labour Party – and he was the best Secretary of State for Northern Ireland we ever had...He belongs to a type that has almost disappeared, from the days when the Labour Party hadn't been taken over by sociology lecturers and focus groups and was still what its name said, the political voice of the working class...Mason turned away from a political solution and set out to govern Northern Ireland wit justice for all; with equality before the law; and, crucially, with republican terrorism treated as a secondary problem, and nothing else.

Geoffrey Wheatcroft, Sunday Telegraph [April 2004]

Mason on...Parliamentary Colleagues

Clem Attlee (1983-67)
'Small in stature, an unlikely looking leader. Balding with a moustache – unusual appearance. Noted for short speeches. Had no time for gossip – did not encourage tea room chat. During my first afternoon, when I was in the tea room, he summoned me to his room – in the days when such a meeting was deemed to be highly important and serious. Clem was at his large desk, peering over the top. I stood there, transfixed. He began: 'Young man you will be here for a long time. I want to give you two pieces of advice: first, specialise, second, keep out of the bar'. Then it was a quick 'good morning'. There were 31 miners MPs in the Commons and he did not want me to join the group. On one occasion, when he spoke at a Yorkshire Miners' Gala, he stayed at my home in Barnsley. When Marjorie took him a morning cup of tea she could not see him at first as he was such a small figure in the bed.'

Hugh Gaitskell (1906-63)
'He gave an impression of being learned. Had leadership qualities. Earnest at the Dispatch Box and also appealing to the majority of Labour backbenchers, indeed a straight man. His honesty was transparent. He warded off the pressures of left wingers. I admired him for that, as I learnt later as the Minister of Defence Equipment and Defence Secretary, warding off the unilateralists, CND, Action for Peace, the Bevanite bloc, Militant Tendency, and a left wing National Executive. When he died in 1963 I lost a good friend and mentor. Politically he was the type I wished to follow. Looking back, many of the Parliamentary Labour Party have regarded him as the Grandfather of the Blair era.'

Aneurin 'Nye' Bevan (1897-1960)
'He was a great orator. He would paint pictures in the sky when he stood to speak. A socialist to his roots. To me, as a government Defence minister he created numerous difficulties but he was genuine, although narrow looking in his political objectives. Bevanism and Bevanites became a creed within the Parliamentary Labour Party – Bevanism did divide the Party. On one occasion, after a Defence debate, he and his supporters on a three-line whip voted against the Party. At the judgement meeting when the recaltricants had the whip withdrawn he turned to me and my friends and shouted 'I will never forgive you!". He stormed out of the Party meeting. Some months later he supported me when I got into bother over a newspaper article, put his arm on my shoulder and said, "There my son, I could not do better than that for you".

Harold Macmillan (1894-1986)
'Flying Mac, like a bird in cartoons. Nothing wrong with him. He wasn't a bad bloke.

Illness affected his career. Aristocratic background. Once sacked half his Cabinet ['Night of the Long Knives']. He came across well.'

Harold Wilson (1916-95)
'A good friend. Although many of us were aware of his 'scheming' – because of the numerous factions he had to control throughout his time – including CND, militants, Bevanites, Action for Peace and indeed a biased National Executive – so there were many balls in the air! He got his Cabinet to the balance that he enjoyed, several key individuals he could rely on. We did not have a lot of trouble, only one or two might challenge him. I did not challenge him often. He retired prematurely, no doubt pressure playing a part. Illness too. As a member of the Cabinet the day he told us that he was retiring I was shocked as most of us were. His staunch deputy, Ted Short, shed tears. I too sat dumbstruck. We were to lose a good leader. He was also a pipeman.'

George Brown (1914-85)
'A two-part man. He had a team of junior ministers under him, looking after the Army, Navy and Air Force. We were ready to assist. In his early days he was a good speaker, a straight man and very friendly with most MPs but towards the end of his parliamentary time what people said was that he had taken to drink. But he had an ailment which if he did have a drink or two he was soon affected. I was always told not to ask him for a drink. They were trying to control it. Very able politician.'

Barbara Castle (1910-2002)
'A fiery Leftie as was well known. Able, but usually went too far. Popular in Labour Party meetings, took notes etc in Cabinet – but this was frowned on by all including Prime Minister Harold Wilson – her Dairies were based on her notes, and she did well out of it. Prayed on Harold Wilson in order to get her own way on ministerial matters.'

Tony Benn (1925-)
'Not recognised within senior government circles as a good minister. Like Barbara Castle, he took notes during Cabinet meetings for his Diaries. At one time or another when we were shuffled in a Cabinet process I sat next to them both – one, Barbara Castle, using shorthand and the other, Benn, in longhand. Warned by Harold Wilson as it was strictly against the rules. Colleagues became concerned about speaking honestly on issues. He played to workers and dreamers – eg, fight for the miners, and yet agreed with a report to close uneconomic coalmines.'

Edward Heath (1916-2005)
'He had a rather dull presentation as a leader, a grey figure. A good man for his party but did not gather many close, friendly lieutenants. His leadership left much to be desired. Heath was not a mixer or leader of the masses. Even his sporting interests took him out of the many inexpensive sports, into yachting and sailing, but he had the right wing style of leadership – but his leadership qualities were of no avail in gathering mass support.'

James Callaghan (1912-2005)
'Sunny Jim! Don't you believe it! A pleasant profile and cheery disposition, yes, but he had steel in his spine. A no nonsense politician but with charm! Very knowledgeable, a good mixer and his leadership was rarely faulted. Chaired Cabinet without fear or favour, with a style stronger than Wilson's. I found one aspect of his leadership a bit frustrating, though. Wilson, during a cabinet shuffle would meet most of those affected. Jim did most of his by telephone.'

Denis Healey (1917-)
'Robust and intelligent. Good at the Dispatch Box. A leader of men – he stood no nonsense from the military or political leaks such as gossip. He had to be convinced at times and it was somewhat wearing to hear his call. Gained much from his straightforward manner. I think all the staff appreciated his strong voice and style. One 'Prime Minister' who we never got but he may have turned the public off. A remarkably good photographer.'

Roy Jenkins (1920-2003)
'For the left of centre Labour Party members he appeared off hand. Not an easy mixer. He had a straight-laced attitude – snooty and understandably had leadership qualities. When I was involved during a postal workers' dispute my help was frowned upon. As Chancellor he knew his job. He strongly desired leadership. Was really a good addition to the hierarchy of the Labour Party. His leadership style might have grated on some of his followers but for his time and type of ministerial office he did well.'

John Prescott (1938-)
'Came into the House of Commons as a young trade unionist. Eager. Wanted to become involved quickly. Gave the impression as a solid Labour MP. Harold Wilson, when he was shadow PM allowed me as shadow President of the Board of Trade to bring good politicians to the front bench and, for shipping, Prescott was my man. I chose him to speak on a shipping bill and his father came to the House to hear him, from the gallery. He did well in his maiden front bench oration. I was his mentor for a short time, visiting the docks with me and attending briefings, really the beginnings of his learning curve, showing good promise.'

Michael Foot (1913-)
'As a politician within the Parliamentary Labour Party and Cabinet colleague, we worked together but not very closely. Yes, he was a socialist democrat but his basic, strongly held views clashed with some – yet he did get to the leadership of the Party. We did not see eye to eye on many issues, ie, on Defence, Party leadership and divisions within the Labour Party. I do remember his duffle coat and did not approve, especially at the Cenotaph, but I understood, he was not a straight jacket. I also attended the Cenotaph services. I had no strong ministerial differences with Michael. He was very left and principled as perceived by many within the PLP and he did become the leader which coincided with the PLP moving to the left.'

Ian Paisley (1926-)
'Dr Doubtful. I could do business with him, especially after our first meeting when he arrived fifteen minutes late. I docked him fifteen minutes off his schedule – he never forgot it. A good consituency MP but a ranter for his causes, indeed I had him arrested after a confrontation with the security officers – at 4 am! He settled down during the recent Northern Ireland talks. I believe cash for the North as part of the peace settlement may have oiled the wheels.'

Margaret Thatcher (1925-)
'I once described her quite publicly as a Cold War Warrior and thought that she might be offended. But she seemed to revel in it. Politically we were poles apart, but during my Northern Ireland experiences and dangers she came to recognise and appreciate our different problems and over time made sure that we shelved our misunderstandings. As a lady leader of a political party she was quite remarkable. We still meet in the corridors of the House of Lords, smile, say hello and occasionally a little more, indeed in her heyday – on one of her rare No 10 parties – she invited my wife and I to attend. We did, not for long. We were a rare couple in that gathering. Yes, a strange example of political differences that are overcome by appreciation of ones personal political problems.'

Neil Kinnock (1942-)
'Born of good stock, a sound socialist education. Leadership material but unfortunately critics described him as a Welsh windbag or a Welsh wizard – but he was undeniably good on the platform. Jealousies abound. Married to Glenys, a lady of especial political ability – a good pairing. They took the political path together very successfully too. Neil led the Party in 1983. He grew into the job and became a real leader; if the Party is transformed today it's largely because of the foundations he laid.'

John Smith (1938-94)
'Good mannered and friendly. An able debater and a quality Cabinet minister, he typified the good heart of the Labour Party. Had a religious streak. I received the news of his passing in the morning at the House of Lords and was shocked and shaken.'

Tony Blair (1953-)
'A most remarkable man as leader of the Party and now recognised as a statesman internationally. He was the best Labour Party leader in my parliamentary time. I was called to see him along with my great friend Lord Lofthouse, who has done so much work on chest disease compensation for coal miners, on 3 May 2007, a few weeks before his retirement as Prime Minister. Tony complimented me on my long political career which began in 1953 when I was 28 and especially for my service in Northern Ireland. We laughed when he reminded me of my first meeting with Clem Attlee when he told me, a small, bald-headed man looking over a huge desk, to specialise and keep out of the bar. Later, on 20 June, I wrote to him, saying that he had given our Party great international status and that he would carry on to become a great world statesman. I sent him one of my ties that I designed for Labour Peers 'just in case!' and received a very pleasant thank you letter by return.

On a pit visit, Mason shares a joke with a group of Barnsley miners. (MA)

Part One

Early Years, 1924-38

'...my earliest childhood memory is of a dour army of men trudging in the thin light of dawn towards the waiting pithead.'

Joseph Mason and his baby son, Roy, outside 1 Jubilee Terrace, Royston, in 1924. (MA)

Life and Times

1924 [22.1] First Labour Government is formed by Ramsey McDonald.
[18.4] Roy Mason born at Royston, near Barnsley.
[7.11] Baldwin ministry begins following Conservative election victory.

1925 [3.12] Boundary between Northern Ireland and Irish Free State agreed.

1926 [26.2] Edna, Roy's sister, born at Carlton, Barnsley.
[1.5] Miners' strike (to 12.11).
[3.5] General strike (to 12.5).

1927 [23.11] Baldwin refuses to meet 200 unemployed Welsh miners.

1929 [-34] Mason at Carlton elementary schools.
[7.6] McDonald forms 2nd Labour Government.
[7.8] Unemployment reaches two million.

1931 [24.8] National Government formed, led by McDonald.
[20.11] Bentley pit disaster, Doncaster, 45 killed.

1934 [-38] Mason at Royston Secondary Boys' School.
[22.9] Gresford (Wrexham) pit disaster, 265 miners killed.

1935 [6.5] King George and Queen Mary's Silver Jubilee, many street parties in Barnsley area.
[7.6] Baldwin is Prime Minister again.
[19.9] North Gawber, Barnsley pit disaster, 19 killed.
[8.10] Clem Attlee is new Labour Party leader.

1936 [11.1] Arthur Scargill born, Worsbrough, near Barnsley.
[28.1] Death of George V.
[11.3] George Orwell arrives in Barnsley, researching his book *The Road to Wigan Pier*.
[15.3] Sir Oswald Mosley and his 'Blackshirts' (British Union of Fascists) march through Barnsley and meet at the Public Hall. Protesting Communist Tommy Degnan is ejected from the meeting.
[6.8] Wharncliffe Woodmoor colliery disaster, 58 killed and Mason is an eyewitness of pit-top scenes.
[5.10] Jarrow Hunger March to London.
[11.12] Abdication radio speech of Edward VIII.

1937 [9.3] George Orwell's The Road to Wigan Pier is published, partly based on lodging in Barnsley, and underground visits to local pits.

[12.5] Coronation of George VI.
[28.5] Neville Chamberlain now leads National Government.

1938 [15.7] Aged 14, Mason is an unemployed school leaver.

Overview

Roy Mason was born on Wednesday 18 April 1924 at 1 Jubilee Terrace, an end terraced house in the village of Royston, a West Riding of Yorkshire mining community situated about four miles north of Barnsley. His parents were Joseph (a coal miner) and Mary Hannah Mason nee McDonald. Coincidentally, Ramsey McDonald had just formed his first Labour government. Mary was a local girl but Joseph was not. A few years earlier, during the Great War, Joseph, probably with his parents, walked over 100 miles from Staffordshire seeking pitwork.

A word of qualification at this point. The Masons' family name ought to have been Smith. Joseph Mason's father, also named Joseph, fought in the Boer War, leaving a pregnant girlfriend, Catherine Mason, at home. Their son was registered as Joseph Mason, a name which was retained even when the couple married. This unusual situation was much appreciated by the Rt Hon Roy Mason MP many years later whose messages and correspondence might not have otherwise been so easily directed to him in the House of Commons. There was only one Mason at Westminster but several Smiths.

The Masons appear to have originally settled in the nearby village of Carlton, in Carlton Terrace (also known as Long Row), a distinctive row of mineworkers' cottages sited next to Carlton Main colliery (soon to be called Wharncliffe Woodmoor 4 & 5). Certainly by 1917, young Joseph Mason was playing football for his local team: Carlton 'Vics' (Victoria) which was made up of young miners living at Long Row. Then, on Christmas Eve 1919, Joseph Mason junior, aged 24, married his Royston sweetheart, Mary Hannah McDonald (22), in Royston parish church. Mary lived at Dove Hill, a small terrace, off Midland Road, Royston, not far from Monckton Colliery where her father, also a miner, probably worked. It seems likely that it was shortly after their marriage that the Masons took lodgings at 1 Jubilee Terrace, their first home.

The developing New Monckton Colliery complex was a great attraction for migrant workers from the Black Country, a Klondyke-style rush which resulted in Royston being known as 'little Staffordshire'. The newcomers brought with them their own distinctive dialect and dry sense of humour. As late as the 1970s, when I taught at Royston Secondary School, the speech of some of the children was certainly different to that experienced in nearby Barnsley.

By 1926, the Masons had moved out of their cramped accommodation in Royston, where they lodged with a family called Shilton, back to Long Row. This coincided with the birth of Roy's sister Edna and the start of the 26-week national miners' strike, so the family would have experienced hard times. However, Long Row, with its working men's club at the end of the street was a typical close-knit mining community where everyone pulled together during adversity. Joseph became a committee man at the club. I've talked to a few elderly miners who were young men during the '26 strike. Hardship was certainly remembered: attending soup kitchens, picking coal from the muckstack and hauling it home on a push-bike, even digging shallow pit shafts. The long hot summer was also appreciated; it was time to forget about the pit and enjoy long walks in the countryside, potter in an allotment and fly pigeons. I guess Joseph did the same.

Long Row, therefore, was where Roy spent his early years, listening to the sound of clogs in the early hours, skylarks in the nearby fields, close to the pit yard where he would soon walk across to work, albeit from a different part of the village. When I was a boy in the 1950s several of my friends lived at Long Row, so I would often go to see them, walking there from old Carlton. It was a place that had great sporting traditions, particularly football and cricket which we played on adjacent pieces of spare land. We fished in the canal and pond and went 'nesting' for birds' eggs in the surrounding countryside. 'Kadgies' (makeshift children's 'cars' cobbled together with bits of timber, old rope and pram wheels) speeded down the quarter-mile street, distracted by the sight and sound of Kilner's ice-cream van. Occasionally we would venture further afield, via the 'monkey tunnel', a subway under the railway, reached through the pit yard, which took us to Cudworth village where there was a park, even an outdoor swimming pool and a cinema.

By the late 1920s, Roy had started school, at Carlton Spring Lane Junior Mixed, situated near St John's Church. About the same time, there was yet another move - or 'flit' as it was known locally: to a council house on a small new development, set slightly away from the village but a short walk to school. Number 3 Manor Street was a smart, three-bedroomed, semi-detached council property with a small garden at the front and a larger, more private one at the back. It was the height of luxury as it also had a bathroom. The old tin bath was redundant. This area, consisting of Manor Street, Wharncliffe Street and Woodmoor Street, was known simply as 'new houses' for many years but nicknamed 'Sticky Top'. One abiding folk theory is that this name was applied by not so lucky locals who saw the new residents as 'stuck-up' in their relatively posh houses and somewhat eminent location. However, it probably originated because of the problems that miners had getting the coal from difficult seams immediately below the area.

Roy transferred to the 'Top' or Senior Boys' School at Carlton Green, across from the growing muckstack of Wharncliffe Woodmoor 1, 2 & 3 Colliery but was unable to fulfil his scholarship ambition, a huge disappointment. When this school closed in 1934 he moved to the new Royston Senior Boys' School where he completed his elementary education.

In 1936, on a grim and dismal August morning, there was an explosion at Wharncliffe Woodmoor 1, 2 & 3 colliery which resulted in the death of 58 miners. As a 12-year-old boy Mason witnessed the aftermath of this terrible day for the village, his old school used as a temporary mortuary. My father was employed as a young miner at the pit at the time and was one of the lucky ones who was not working on that fateful night shift.

The new house was a great improvement but times were extremely hard in mining communities. Depression in the coal trade was particularly bad in South Yorkshire, most miners only working three shifts a week, grateful to claim dole towards the shortfall. Working a fourth shift would have resulted in loss of benefit so it is not surprising that miners used strategies to avoid this situation at all costs. To help make ends meet the Masons took in a lodger, Tom Stevenson. Tom built a crystal radio set so, for the first time, they could also listen to music and hear news broadcasts.

Roy's spare time activities were considerable and probably helped mould his future more than any formal education. This included attendance at St John's parish church, Carlton, four times on Sundays, singing in the choir. Then there was the Scouts, the 34th Royston Methodists. The challenges of completing a range of activities for proficiency badges and awards were met with enthusiasm and success, Roy eventually becoming a First Class King's Scout. Most enjoyable of all was camping in the open air, an activity he enjoyed so much that he set up his tent, sometimes on his own, in Notton Park, a patch of ancient woodland on the outskirts of Royston, spending weekends under canvas.

Roy Mason left Royston Secondary Boys' School in the summer of 1938. He was fourteen. He enjoyed school but did not work 'especially hard' in view of a predicable future down the mine; and yet even that prospect had no immediate outcome. There were no jobs. After all, this period was what one old Yorkshire miner described to me as the 'wicked thirties', the depression. Poverty was widespread. Families existed on the breadline. Fashionable young men's summer slacks could be bought from town for fifteen shillings (75p) but young Mason could not afford any, as his dole money had to be handed over to help the family budget. Within a few weeks details of Neville Chamberlain's Munich Agreement, including his 'peace for our time' comment, were heard on Tom Stevenson's crystal set at 3 Manor Street and in cinemas, all too soon dashed by Hitler's invasion of Prague. A memorable chapter in Roy Mason's life began.

Joseph Mason, seated, with the ball at his feet, as captain of Carlton Vics (Victoria) in season 1917-18. Probably photographed at Carlton Main Working Men's Club, the players are sporting a small rosette, perhaps an indication of league or cup success. The dog looks an impressive mascot. (MA)

Registration District Barnsley

1924. **Birth in the Sub-district of** Darton **in the** County of York

Columns:- 1		2	3	4	5	6	7	8	9	10
No.	When and where born	Name, if any	Sex	Name, and surname of father	Name, surname and maiden surname of mother	Occupation of father	Signature, description, and residence of informant	When registered	Signature of registrar	Name entered after registration
449	Eighteenth April 1924 1 Jubilee Terrace Midland Road Royston U D	Roy	Boy	Joseph MASON	Mary Ann MASON Formerly McDONALD	Collier (Hewer)	Joseph Mason Father 1 Jubilee Terrace Midland Road Royston Barnsley	Twelfth May 1924	J H Norbury Registrar	

Roy Mason's birth was registered at Darton on 12 May 1924 by his father, Joseph, who is described as a collier or hewer. (Registration of Births, Marriage and Deaths, Barnsley Town Hall)

Extracting coal with a pick, standing in water, wearing shorts and stripped to the waist in the old 'hand-got' and piecework days was an extremely hard and dangerous job, even for a young collier. (BEC)

Midland Road, Royston, as Joseph and Mary Mason would have remembered. Formerly Senior Lane, it was renamed after the Midland Railway which ran by Monckton pit. A small group of locals stand between a confectioner's and barber's shop. In the distance a man has just walked by the Palace Cinema. (Old Barnsley)

This extract from a large-scale map dated 1909 shows the location of Jubilee Terrace, looking a little isolated, accessed either by a footpath or track towards the end of Midland Road. The cottages, two-up, two-down and long demolished were probably built in Queen Victoria's jubilee year of 1887. The map also shows the close proximity of Dove Hill, where Mary Mason (nee McDonald) previously lived. (Courtesy of the Ordnance Survey)

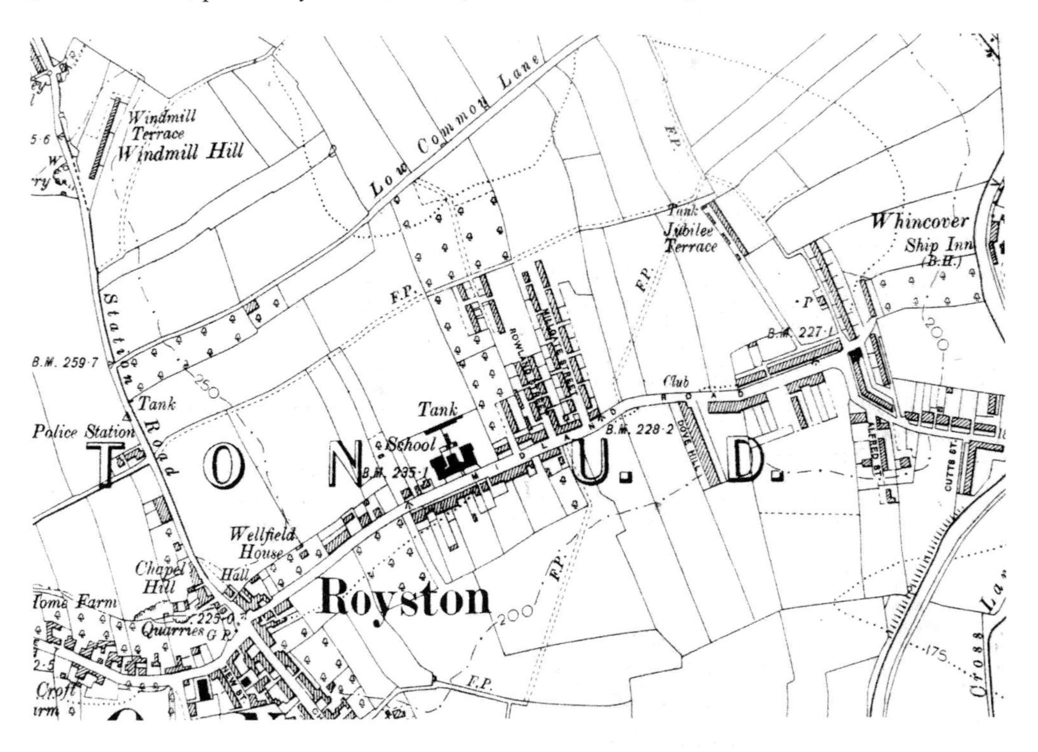

Dove Hill still exists, seen here in the 1970s, a graduated terrace of over 20 cottages, sloping down from Midland Road, a working men's club sited at the upper end. (BEC)

This photograph of Strawberry Gardens, situated fairly close to Jubilee Terrace, shows typical working-class housing, yards and middens. Even in the 1970s, the odd tin bath could be seen hung outside back doors. Miners came home in their 'pit muck'. Vermin such as 'blackclocks' (beetles) were commonplace. Pit clothes left drying overnight, needed to be shaken the next morning. The name Strawberry Gardens may seem a little inept but market gardens once thrived in the area. (BEC)

Sunk in 1875, what became known as New Monckton Collieries (1 & 2 and 4 & 5) was an industrial complex of considerable scale by the 1920s and 1930s, incorporating a coke and chemical works and a brick-making plant. One of the largest mines in Yorkshire, it employed almost 4,000 men in its heyday, including my grandfathers. It closed in 1966 but the processing plant still operates. (Old Barnsley)

Royston Urban District Council in 1925. On the front row, third from the left, is a young councillor, Horace Holmes who became MP for the Hemsworth constituency (which then included Royston) following the death of George Griffiths (seated to Horace's left), in 1946. It was Holmes, a former Monckton miner and union official, who introduced the new Barnsley MP, Roy Mason, to the Commons in 1953. (Howard Jones)

Joseph Mason would have recognised this early image of Long Row. The chap wearing the bowler looks rather officious and maybe the other man on the pavement was the knocker-up. In May 1878, 60 brick and stone cottages were erected here at a cost of £152 each for a weekly rent of 4s 6d (stone) and 4s 6d (brick). By 1890 the main row had been extended to almost 90 properties, including a working men's club. Mary baked her own bread and assembled Joseph's 'snap', consisting of lard or dripping and a bottle of water. Long Row was demolished in 1970. (Old Barnsley)

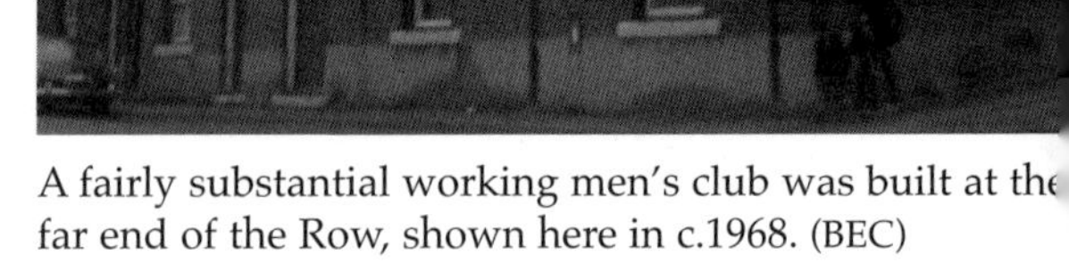

A fairly substantial working men's club was built at the far end of the Row, shown here in c.1968. (BEC)

This view, from the direction of Wharncliffe Woodmoor 4 & 5 Colliery yard, shows Long Row and Stone Row just before demolition. The shorter and higher specification Stone Row was built for the pit 'officials', mainly deputies and overmen. (BEC)

This rare image shows Roy and his sister Edna (b.26 February 1926) outside the front door of their new house, 3 Manor Street, Carlton, in about 1930. (MA)

Both Carlton Terrace and Manor Street (off Fish Dam Lane) can be seen on this large-scale map dating from c.1930. It was but a short walk down Mill Lane and over the canal bridge to reach Carlton Main (Wharncliffe Woodmoor 4 & 5 colliery). Spring Lane school can also be seen, by the road junction. (Courtesy of the Ordnance Survey)

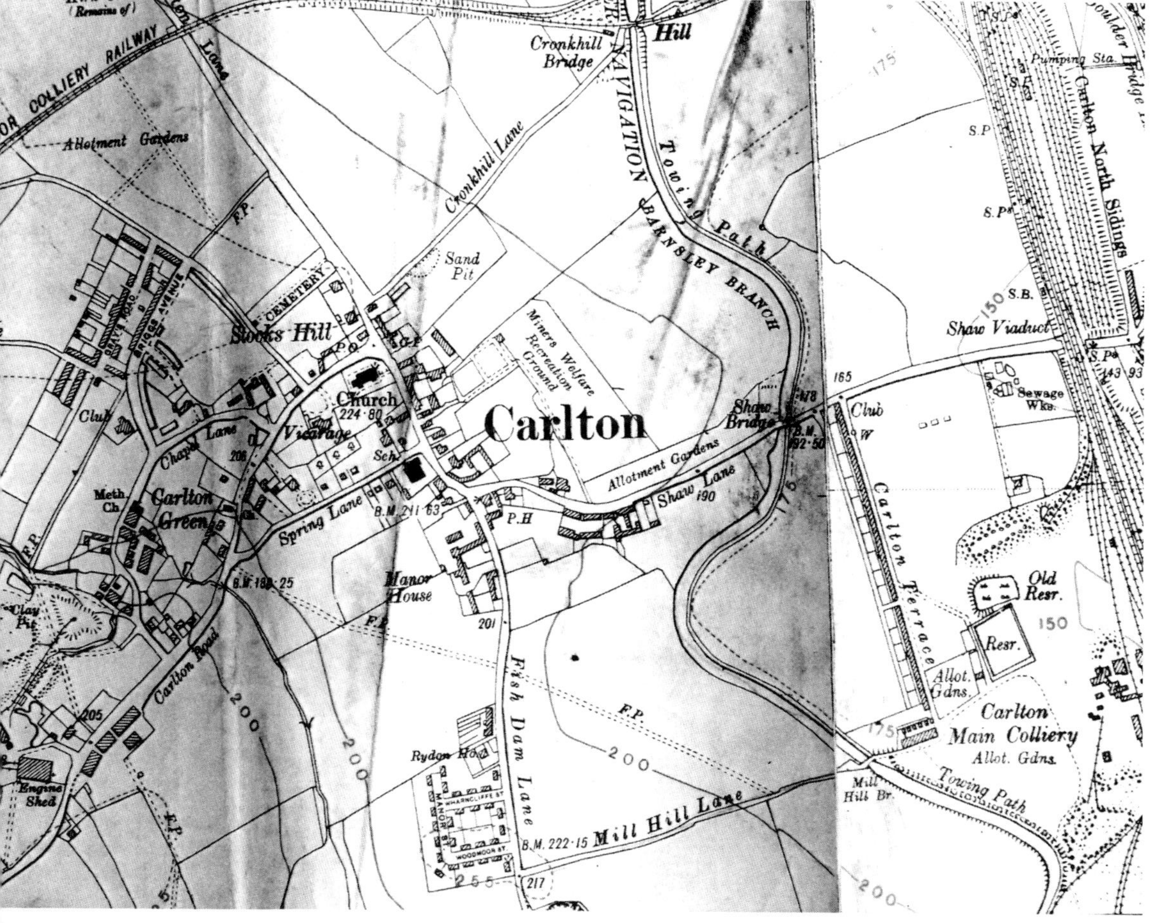

Class of c. 1930/31 assembled for the school photographer at the Spring Lane side of Carlton Junior Mixed. Roy Mason is in the 2nd row from the back, third from the left. He is wearing a monitor's ribbon, an early sign of responsibility. (MA)

Carlton Primary School (formerly Spring Lane Junior Mixed) during its demolition in 1972. Mining subsidence caused structural problems during the post-war period, though a new infants' extension was built in 1953. The temporary looking structure across the school yard was the canteen and assembly hall. I remember it well. (BEC)

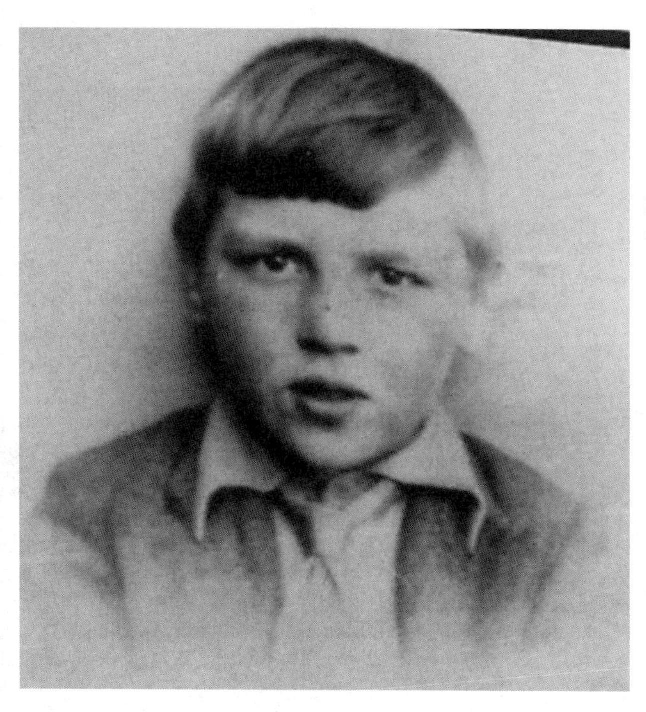

Schoolboy Mason, looking characteristically smart, c.1932. (MA)

Crowds waiting anxiously outside the old Senior School at Carlton Green on 6 August 1936 where a temporary mortuary was set up following the terrible disaster at Wharncliffe Woodmoor 1,2 & 3 colliery in which 58 men lost their lives. The explosion in the Lidgett seam occurred under fields a short walk away, off Laithes Lane. This was part of the scene witnessed by twelve-year-old Roy Mason. (BEC)

The new Royston Modern School (now Royston High School) which had separate departments (two blocks) for boys and girls when Roy Mason attended from c.1934 to 1938. The headmaster of the boys' school was George F Laycock. (BEC)

The staff and caretaker (far right) of Royston Senior Boys' School pictured in the 1930s. Back row (L to R): Ronald Southern, -?-, John W Davey, Gwilym Jones, -?- and caretaker. Front Row (L-R): Arnold Green, Arthur Wilson and -?-. Roy Mason has particular memories of daydreaming and whispering to friends at the back of 'fierce' (and 6ft 2 inch tall) Mr Davey's art and crafts class. The outcome was ten blows on the backside with a paint palette – pain and humiliation in front of his mates. Roy remembers storming back to his seat, kicking a chair over in the process, only to receive ten more whacks for losing his temper. Dad, all 5 ft. 7 in. of him came to protest but to no avail. (BEC)

Inside St John the Evangelist's church, Carlton, in the paraffin lighting days. This was where Roy Mason was a young chorister, attending up to four times on Sundays during Revd Norman King's ministry. (BEC)

Scouting activities in Notton Park, a woodland area on the outskirts of Royston.

Lord Mason makes a nostalgic return visit to 3 Manor Street, Carlton in May 2007. (BEC)

In the back garden of 3 Manor Street with present occupant, Mrs Thelma McLoughlan, who has lived there for 40 years. (BEC)

Part Two

Miner and Union Man
1938-52

'Working underground was hard, dirty and dangerous...'

At home at the end of a shift: young miner Roy Mason in his pit clothes, sat on the back door steps of his 'prefab' (prefabricated bungalow), 292 Carlton Road, Smithies in c.1950. (MA)

Life and Times

Year	Date	Event
1938	[7]	Roy Mason is 'on the dole'.
	[3.9]	Chamberlain's 'Peace for our time' agreement with Adolf Hitler proclaimed.
	[9]	Mason starts work as a trainee Fitter, Wharncliffe Woodmoor 4&5 Colliery, Carlton, near Barnsley.
	[9]	Mason joins Yorkshire Miners' Union (NUM from 1944).
1939	[31.8]	Evacuation of children from town and cities.
	[3.9]	War is declared between Britain and Germany.
	[10.9]	Mason joins his local Air Training Corps where he meets Marjorie Sowden.
1940	[8.1]	Food rationing in Britain.
	[10.5]	Churchill leads National Government.
	[15.9]	Battle of Britain ends with British victory.
1941	[11.5]	Chamber of House of Commons destroyed by German bombing raid.
1942	[17.2]	Barnsley Main pit disaster, 12 killed.
	[3.6]	Government takes over coal mines.
	[15.11]	Church bells ring for El Alemein victory.
1943		Mason joins the Carlton Ward of the Labour Party.
	[2.12]	'Bevin Boys' called up to work in coal mines.
1944		Death of Roy Mason's mother, Mary Mason, aged 46.
		Women's Land Army now has 80,000 recruits, including Marjorie Sowden.
	[6.6]	D-Day invasion.
1945	[8.5]	End of Second World War against Germany.
	[26.7]	Clem Attlee is new Labour Prime Minister.
	[2.9]	Japan surrenders.
	[20.10]	Mason marries Marjorie Sowden, daughter of a railway worker, Royston Parish Church, near Barnsley.
1947(-53)		Mason is elected NUM Branch Official (Wharncliffe Woodmoor 4 & 5 Colliery).
	[1.1]	Vesting Day: nationalisation of coal mines.
	[4.7]	Birth of Roy and Marjorie's Mason's daughter, Susan.
	[21.6]	Prime Minister Attlee in Barnsley.
	[29.9]	Harold Wilson joins the Cabinet at the age of 31.
	[20.11]	Princess Elizabeth marries Prince Philip.

1948	[5.7]	National Health Service starts.
1949(-53)		Mason is elected to Yorkshire Miners' Council.
1950	[23.2]	Labour retain power in General Election but with a small majority.
	[28.9]	Cresswell pit disaster, Debyshire, 80 miners killed.
1951	[9]	Mason gains TUC Scholarship, London School of Economics.
	[3.5]	Festival of Britain
	[26.10]	Churchill is Prime Minister again.
1952		Mason is Parliamentary Candidate for Bridlington
	[6.2]	Accession of Queen Elizabeth II.

Overview

This part of the book covers Roy Mason's formative teenage years as a pit lad during wartime to the eve of his nomination for the parliamentary consituency of Barnsley at the age of 28. They were difficult years. Low points are easy to find: as a school leaver on the dole at 14; the shock of experiencing first-hand what work was really like underground in a Yorkshire coal mine; witnessing a dead miner being carried out of the pit on his second shift; buried in a roof-fall on two occasions and injured on another; his father carried out of the same mine following yet another accident, becoming an invalid and suffering from the long-term effects of mining; a hard-working mother dying prematurely; having to live in lodgings and in a community where poverty was widespread; suffering injustices associated with pay and conditions; and refused admission to serve in the RAF. But all these adversities undoubtedly contributed to the making of the man and occupied many aspects of his future public life: speaking and campaigning on behalf of the miners and disadvantaged individuals and groups; not standing for social injustice and generally being both fair and firm on a whole range of issues throughout his later political career. Mason's personal qualities of hard work, sound research, honesty and an ability to communicate with knowledge and eloquence to a wide audience later endeared him to become one of the most respected members of the Harold Wilson and Jim Callaghan governments.

In the 1930s, 14-year-old lads were still allowed to work underground on their first day of employment, taken to the most hazardous parts of a mine, without any proper training and given minimum supervision. Safety had improved over the years due to more effective legislation and a better system of inspection but mining continued to be a dangerous occupation. If anything, the demand for coal during the war increased the chances of serious accidents. On his second shift at Wharncliffe Woodmoor 4 & 5 pit Roy witnessed a dead miner being carried out of the workings - symbolically feet first, on a stretcher. It was the moment, he told me 'that my childhood ended'. Not long afterwards Mason himself experienced the first of three accidents, buried in a roof-fall and taken to hospital. He survived but one of his workmates did not. Later, Joseph Mason, Roy's father, was carried out of his pit 'more dead than alive', and developed rheumatic fever, becoming an invalid but having to work as a colliery surface labourer for the remainder of his working life. The death of Roy's mother, Mary, in 1944, at the age of 46, was a devastating blow. Roy became the main family wage earner.

Dreadful working conditions and terrible accidents occurred when piecework prevailed. Coal was in demand again but it was at a huge human cost. During the war 5,400 men and boys were killed in British coal mines. The strategic importance of coal was such that coalmining was a reserved occupation and young men known as Bevin Boys were conscripted into the workforce. Their contribution has only recently been fully and officially recognised thanks mostly to Lord Mason's tireless campaigns over many years. He never forgot them.

Roy Mason took his father's advice to join the Union when he started work and, spurred on by the Labour general election victory of 1945, soon became a young representative for his pit and member of the local Labour Party. He had also become increasingly competent at his job as an underground fitter and improved his prospects by attending day-release and evening classes for his deputy's 'ticket'.

However, the most important event of Roy Mason's life took place in election year when he married his long-term sweetheart, a Land Army girl, Marjorie Sowden. Times were hard for the young couple, living in lodgings and later in a council prefab. It would have been easy for Roy to abandon his further education and growing interest in trade union and politics but Marjorie supported him, as she has done in all their married life.

In 1947, the year of the birth of the Masons' first daughter, Susan, Roy also experienced first-hand another type of euphoria when coal mines were nationalised but was wise to realise that much work was still to be done to fight for better conditions of employment.

Elected on the Yorkshire Miners' Council, Roy gained a TUC scholarship to the London School of Economics in 1951, travelling to see Marjorie and his infant daughter as often as he could get a lift home - via a relative's lorry.

Although at the time he had no intention of pursuing a career in public life, it was a direction that became increasingly evident. Elected on the Yorkshire Miners' Parliamentary Panel, in 1952 he was selected by the local Labour Party as parliamentary candidate for the Yorkshire holiday town of Bridlington. However, any opportunity to be considered for a vacant mining constituency was made clear and agreed. The opportunity came quicker than expected and the road to Westminster began on more familiar ground, in his home town of Barnsley.

After a short period 'on the dole' 14-year-old Roy Mason, all 5ft 2in of him, started work at Wharncliffe Woodmoor 4 & 5 colliery in the autumn of 1938. This photograph was taken in July 1970 when the pit closed. More than 1,500 men were once employed here but one or two of the older 'last shifters' may remember Roy Mason as a young underground fitter more than twenty years earlier. (Thelma Carnevale/BEC)

Once out of the cage he realised for the first time that there were advantages of being only 5ft 2in tall. The journey to work had hardly begun: 'In front of us stretched the tunnel to the coalface, low and narrow, full of clamour and activity and the screech of tubs on rails...Deeper and deeper we went, sometimes bent double, heading always towards the noise ahead, squeezing past miners and pit props and secondary tunnels...at the Beamshaw seam, 1ft 6in of coal, the noise was overwhelming – I was on my belly, crawling through, coughing in the swirling dust...Men were ahead of me and around me, lying on their sides, contorted, black with muck, stripped to the waist, cutting and hacking with picks, sweating, tearing out the coal...' The roadway may not have been quite as decrepit as this one, but no less daunting. The first sight of the coalface for a 14-year-old must have been an unforgettable one. This period image was taken from the gob or waste side, men shovelling coal on to a moving conveyor belt. Each collier had his stint (length of face) to complete during the shift. (BEC)

Getting to the bottom of the shaft for the first time was unforgettable for most young lads and Roy's experience was no exception: 'Suddenly the cage began to drop...a terrifying rate of descent which left my stomach desperately trying to catch up. Down and down we plunged into darkness...Then I staggered as the cage jerked to an abrupt halt.' (BEC)

Under the supervision of fitter Joe Newman, Roy began to learn the trade of repairing and maintaining longwall coal-cutting machines which had to be kept working as men would lose their wages under the piecework system. This example was photographed by Irvin Harris at Woolley Colliery in 1948. (BEC)

On his second morning, Roy's baptism to mining was complete when he witnessed a dead miner hurried on a stretcher to the cage. 'I think', he said, 'that was the moment my childhood ended'. It wasn't long before he experienced an accident at first hand, stretchered out of the pit, following a roof fall: '... a vast slab crashed on its end, toppled and slammed into me. I was laid out, helpless, unable to move...in complete darkness...I could hear groans. I screamed for help...at last my fellow miners were around me, grunting and heaving to move the rock which had me trapped.' Two other men were also buried in the rock fall, one seriously injured and the other - whose warning shout may have saved Roy - killed. The photograph showing a dead miner being carried out of Barnsley Main following an explosion in which 8 other men died, in 1947. (BEC)

Roy was taken to Barnsley's Beckett Hospital following his accident but released after a medical examination. Typically, he was at work the next day. He could not afford to miss a day's pay. There was no compensation. In a second accident, when he was alone, repairing a coal-cutting machine, he was buried by fallen rocks, just escaping before the entire roof caved in; and once more taken by ambulance to Beckett's. Again, he returned to work the following day. On a third occasion Roy was temporarily concussed when a metal key from a machine he was repairing struck him on the head. This time a brief examination and the recommendation of 'a good night's sleep' was given in the first aid room on the surface. (BEC)

As a teenage miner it was not surprising that Roy Mason found some solace at continuing his activities with the Scouts. Here he is, outside his Manor Street home. His much decorated shirt, seen in the detailed image, is now on display along with other Mason memorabilia in Cawthorne's Victorian village museum. (MA)

Like most people in the 1930s, going to the 'pictures' was a great means of escape. It could be a trip to the Palace or Ace in Carlton, or maybe to the plush Ritz in town with its Wurlitzer organ. The Rock at nearby Cudworth, seen here, was more basic but a popular venue for young courting couples. (Chris & Pearl Sharp/Old Barnsley)

Still only aged 14, Roy Mason joined the local Air Training Corp at Royston after the outbreak of war and by 1944 was promoted to cadet flight sergeant. (MA)

It was whilst in the ATC that young Mason started courting Marjorie Sowden. She was a member of the Girls' Training Corp who shared the same cadet hut as Roy at Royston Secondary, Roy's old school. Born in Bradford, the daughter of a railwayman, she had moved to Normanton, near Wakefield at the age of three and later to Royston when the new railway sheds were built. Leaving Normanton Girls' High School, Marjorie worked locally as a nursery assistant but joined the Women's Land Army for about 18 months during the war, working in Huntingdonshire. There, she drove tractors for muck spreading, picked potatoes and did various other 'unladylike' jobs much to the surprise of older men on the farm. The photograph of Marjorie shows her as a Land Army girl, c. 1944.

Back at Wharncliffe Woodmoor 4 & 5 pit, Roy Mason was becoming more competent as a fitter, his father, Joseph moving from Monckton to work at the same colliery. To help the war effort, conscripted young lads known as Bevin Boys were also deployed there. Sung to the tune of Paper Doll, this song extract encapsulates one aspect of the 'call-up' age lads' problems:

As I walked down the street the other day,
A damsel turned to me and she did say:
'Why aren't you in khaki or navy blue
And fighting for your country like other boys do?'
I turned to her and this I did reply.
The answer nearly made the poor girl cry!
'The army I have tried to join.
But Bevin sent me down the mine
And left me with a broken heart.' (MA)

Unable to be recruited to the RAF because of coalmining's status as a reserve occupation, Roy had already started night school classes at Barnsley Mining and Technical College in order to improve his qualifications, eventually obtaining his deputy's certificate, though it was never used. It was here that Roy also embarked on a day-release and evening mechanical engineering course. (BEC)

Towards the end of the war, ill-fortune befell the Mason family. Joseph Mason, worn out by hard pit-work and looking a lot older than someone in his late forties, had a terrible accident at the mine, leaving him crippled and needing home nursing. But his wife Mary was already terminally ill with cancer. In practical terms, Roy Mason was now the breadwinner. Mary Mason died, aged 46, in 1944. (MA)

here are offences relating to falsifying or altering a certificate
ossessing a false certificate. ©Crown copyright

CERTIFIED COPY of an  **ENTRY OF MARRIAGE**
Pursuant to the Marriage Act 1949

WARNING: A CERTIFICATE IS NOT EVIDENCE OF IDENTITY.
(Printed by the authority of the Registrar Gene

Registration District Barnsley

19 45. Marriage solemnized at the Parish Church of Royston in the Par... in the County of York.

1 When Married.	2 Name and Surname.	3 Age.	4 Condition.	5 Rank or Profession.	6 Residence at the time of Marriage.	7 Father's Name and Surname.	8 Rank or Professi... Father.
20th day of October 1945	Roy Mason	21	Bachelor	Colliery Fitter	3. Manor Street. Carlton	Joseph Mason	Miner
	Marjorie Sowden	20	Spinster	Women's Land Army	98, Cross Lane, Royston	Ernest Sowden	Railwaym...

...d in the Parish Church according to the Rites and Ceremonies of the Established Church by ... or after banns by ...

...arriage ...mnized ...n us, Roy Mason. Marjorie Sowden

in the Presence of us, Alfred James Armstrong Annie Macdonald

John G. Seebold Vicar

...fied to be a true copy of an entry in a register in my custody, Erin Hennessey Deputy Superintendent Registrar

'...the best and wisest decision of my life'. Roy Mason, aged 21 and Marjorie Sowden, 20 were married at St John's parish church, Royston on 20 October 1945. Their registration certificate shows Roy's rank or profession as 'Colliery Fitter' whilst Marjorie was still in the Women's Land Army. Rev John Seebold presided.

This view of Royston church was the work of local photographer J L Wood, taken in the 1920s or 1930s. The shock of Roy's mother's death was an important factor in deciding to marry. Courting throughout the war years, the end of hostilities was also a most opportune time for the couple to wed. But there was no money for a professional photographer to record the occasion. (BEC)

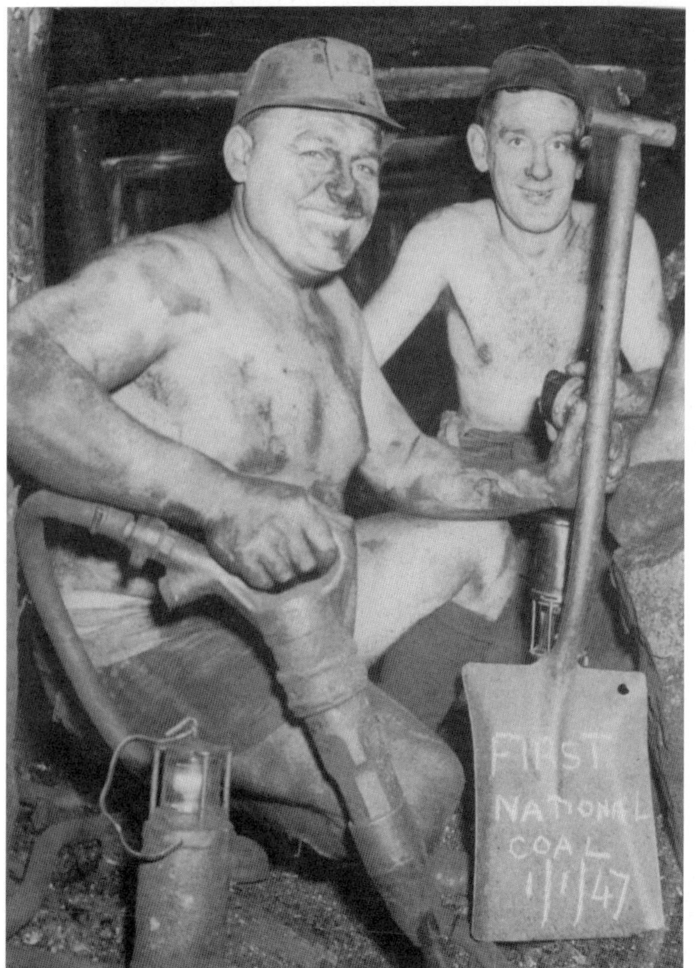

The great problem for most newly married couples after the war - and there were lots of them – was finding somewhere to live. For many it was lodgings, often with parents. The Masons lived at 3 Manor Street, along with Roy's disabled father Joseph and sister Edna (who worked at the Co-op). In 1947, the birth of their first child, Susan, added to the overcrowding so the young family moved across the street, to Mr & Mrs Frank Taylor's house, seen here on a nostalgic trip back to the property in 2007. (BEC)

The nationalisation of the pits took place on 1 January 1947. Known as Vesting Day, it was a memorable occasion for underground fitter Roy Mason. Miners carried on working as usual, in 980 collieries 'managed by the National Coal Board on behalf of the people'. The coal owners were paid the sum of £164,600,000 in compensation. Rightly, the NUM expected better, safer working conditions and improved pay. Pit baths and canteens were certainly appreciated but it was not a magic transformation and absenteeism continued to be a problem. (BEC)

A few months after nationalisation, on 21 June 1947, Prime Minister Clement Attlee (2nd left, front) and Minister of Fuel and Power Emmanuel 'Manny' Shinwell (far right, front) were in Barnsley as speakers at the Yorkshire Miners' Gala. They were given a civic reception at the Town Hall, welcomed by Mayor Charles Bentley and Town Clerk Adam Gilfillan. Shortly afterwards Shinwell was replaced by Hugh Gaitskell who introduced a 6 for 5 days' pay incentive as a tactic against absenteeism. This, however, discriminated against young day-release miners like Roy Mason who missed out because of their technical studies. (BEC)

A workman enjoys a pint of Barnsley Bitter at the Sportsman Inn at Smithies, near Barnsley. Roy Mason attended twice-monthly NUM committee meetings here following his election as a representative for his pit in 1947. (BEC)

Roy Mason raised the injustice of the new pay system at NUM branch level, speaking to several officials, including the militant local Communist delegate to the Yorkshire Miners' Council, Tommy Degnam, seen here in later life (centre of the picture). Representation was to no avail but a tenacious appeal to Hemsworth MP Horace Holmes was an astute move. Holmes was PPS (Parliamentary Private Secretary) to Gaitskell who took on board Mason's complaint, amending the new national bonus scheme. It was Holmes who introduced Mason to the Commons a few years later while Labour leader Hugh Gaitskell soon became the young Barnsley MP's mentor and family friend. (BEC)

Now active in his local (Carlton Ward) Labour Party, Roy Mason was successful in being elected a Delegate to the Yorkshire Miners' Council (YMC), Tommy Degnam strategically standing down, becoming Secretary instead. The NUM's Yorkshire headquarters in Barnsley now became a regular place for Mason to attend meetings. (BEC)

Roy Mason, in his early twenties, excited by the prospect of the new post-war Attlee government, had become involved in local politics through the Carlton Ward Labour Party, as well as trade union representation. Even Westminster was not out of reach when he was voted on the parliamentary panel of the YMC. This large group photograph was taken a few years later, in 1951, probably at Bingley College, when Mason attended an NUM summer school. He is standing on the third row from the front, sixth from the right. (MA)

In 1951 Roy Mason won a TUC scholarship and spent a year at the London School of Economics, coming home to see Marjorie and daughter Susan as often as he could. The family had now moved to their first rented property, a prefab (prefabricated bungalow), 292 Carlton Road, Smithies. This photograph, dating from the 1960s, shows typical prefabs in this area. (BEC)

The Masons struggled to make ends meet when Roy was studying in London, in what he later described as 'the strangest year of my life'. Even with Marjorie working part-time at Woolworth's, Christmas was grim, unable to buy a present for daughter Susan. At the Yorkshire NUM offices Roy had a meeting with one of the most respected figures in the Union, President Joe Hall. Joe gave him £5 (then a large white currency note) which alleviated the situation, a piece of generosity he never forgot. (BEC)

Bridlington harbour, full of working-class holidaymakers in 1952; but, politically speaking, this was True Blue territory when Roy Mason was nominated as the Labour Party candidate. However, unexpected political developments in Barnsley, later the same year, were to result in a nomination for the safe Barnsley seat, and the world of Westminster soon beckoned. (BEC)

From a boy, Roy Mason has supported his local professional football club, Barnsley. Here are his heroes of 1950/51 season which included such great players as Tommy Taylor (later Manchester United and England, tragically killed in the Munich air disaster) and Danny Blanchflower (Irish international and later captain of Tottenham Hotspur). Back Row (L-R): Danny Blanchflower, Herbert Glover, Eddie Bannister, Pat Kelly, Gordon Pallister and Jimmy Baxter. Front row (L-R): Gavin Smith, Eddie McMorran, Cec McCormack, Tommy Taylor and Johnny Kelly. (BEC)

Part Three

Young MP
1953-63

'Not many people can say they were floored in the Chamber by Churchill!'

Following his election as MP for Barnsley, Roy Mason was introduced to the House of Commons on 14 April 1953 by his old mining friend from Royston, Horace Holmes, who was the Labour MP for Hemsworth consituency and the Yorkshire Whip. The lady on the right is Mrs Holmes. The photograph was taken on the members' terrace, to commemorate the occasion. (MA)

Life and Times

1952/3		Mason selected as NUM parliamentary candidate.
		Mason selected as official Labour Party candidate.
1953	[31.3]	Barnsley by-election: Mason elected with a majority of 18,378.
	[14.4]	Mason's introduction to the House.
	[2.6]	Coronation of Elizabeth II.
	[7.5]	Mason's maiden speech in House of Commons.
1955	[4.3]	Birth of Jill Diane Mason, daughter of Roy and Marjorie.
	[6.4]	Sir Anthony Eden is Prime Minister following Churchill's resignation.
	[27.5]	General Election: Mason is returned with a majority of 15, 047. Conservatives win overall.
	[14.12]	Hugh Gaitskill elected as Labour Party leader.
1956		Mason with parliamentary delegation to the Gold Coast (Ghana).
	[23.5]	Calder Hall nuclear power station, the first in Britain, operational.
	[16.11]	Suez crisis deepens.
1957	[10.1]	Harold Macmillan becomes Prime Minister.
	[6.3]	Ghana becomes first British colony in Africa to gain independence.
	[25.3]	Treaty of Rome creates 'Common Market'.
	[20.7]	Macmillan's 'never had it so good' speech in Bradford.
1958	[6.2]	Manchester United 'Busby Babes' disaster, fatalities include former Barnsley player Tommy Taylor and Wombwell-born Mark Jones.
	[8.6]	Death of Joseph Mason (Roy's father), aged 63.
	[9.10]	General Election: Mason returned with a majority of 27,376. Conservatives win overall.
	[-1964]	Mason appointed Labour spokesperson on Defence & Post Office matters.
1960	[2]	Mason with parliamentary delegation to Rhodesia & Nyasaland.
	[3.11]	Gaitskell fights off Wilson's leadership bid.
1961	[12.4]	Yuri Gagarin of the Soviet Union becomes the first man to fly in space.
	[17.9]	'Ban the Bomb' demonstrations in London.
1962	[20.2]	John Glenn becomes first American to obit the earth.
	[6]	Mason with Labour Party delegation to the Berlin Wall.
	[3.10]	Labour Party votes for unilateral nuclear disarmament despite embattled leader Gaitskell's emotive 'fight again to save the party I love' speech.
	[28.10]	End of Cuban missile crisis.

1963 [18.1] Death of Hugh Gaitskell.
[14.2] Harold Wilson elected as Labour Leader.
[5.6] John Profumo resigns from the Government and from Parliament after admitting he lied to the Commons re Christine Keeler.
[1.10] Wilson's 'scientific revolution' speech at the Labour Party conference.
[22.11] Assassination of US President John Kennedy.

Overview

This early but important period of Roy Mason's political and personal life covers the eleven years from his nomination as a parliamentary candidate for the Barnsley Division of the Labour Party to the death of his friend and mentor Hugh Gaitskell.

The achievements of Attlee's great reforming government between 1945 and 1951 were massive, affecting the lives of millions of people of all ages. At home, great industries such as coal, railways and steel were nationalised, the National Health Service began and a start was made to build new houses and new, better quality, schools.

Abroad, the move to withdraw from colonial territories, beginning with India and moving towards Africa and the Middle East coincided with Britain becoming an important member of the Atlantic Alliance during what became known as the Cold War. Mason's international experience began with a visit to the Gold Coast in 1956, the first black colony to become independent as the republic of Ghana. Later he was also able to visit Northern Rhodesia (Zambia) and witness the emerging Berlin Wall. During the Suez crisis of 1956, when British and French troops, in collaboration with Israel, invaded the Canal Zone, Mason, like most of his Labour colleagues (and a few Conservatives) considered the action a big mistake, 'without proper parliamentary approval' and recalled impassioned and convincing speeches by Gaitskell in the Commons. 'It was,' he told me, 'the downfall of Prime Minister Eden'.

When Mason entered parliament in the spring of 1953 Winston Churchill, the greatest Englishman alive, was a grand old man of 79 and in the second year of his last premiership. On 2 June, Westminster Abbey was the scene of the coronation of Queen Elizabeth II, the capital's greatest celebration since the end of the Second World War. The young Barnsley MP gave up his place in the Abbey in favour of an outside seat so that his wife Marjorie and daughter Susan could be together. The Coronation gave a massive boost to television. In Carlton village I can just remember visiting my great aunt's house, along with half of our street, to watch the event live on a small TV that she had specially bought.

Mason's early years as a 'collier MP' occurred in the uneasy wake of the 1952 Clean Air Act, a landmark piece of legislation intended to reduce and eradicate the smogs and pea-souper fogs that prevailed in large urban and industrial areas. It also stopped people from burning coal in favour of smokeless forms of energy. This was also a decade when government and local authorities carried out massive slum clearance schemes, getting rid of the kind of back-to-back, two-up, two-down housing that Mason and his family had experienced first-hand.

In 1954, the British aviation industry had great hopes for the Comet but a series of mysterious crashes undermined its international standing. Mason's interest in the avaition and leisure industry was formative at this time.

It was as an opposition MP that the young Labour man from Barnsley would spend his first decade in parliament, in the twilight era of Clem Attlee and the troubled leadership of Hugh Gaitskell. This was a period recently described by Andrew Marr as 'a golden-tinted era of lost content...truly a different country' (Marr, 115). A sea of caps and hats dominanted the terraces of Oakwell, Barnsley's football ground - on a good day. Schoolboys wore short trousers. Great saddness came on 6 February 1958 when two Barnsley-born 'Busby Babes', Tommy Taylor and Mark Jones, died in the Munich plane disaster.

The 1950s was also the dawn of the atomic age. Calder Hall, the world's first nuclear power station opened in 1956. But nuclear power was later to be a great political and loyalty test for the coalfield MP.

Anthony Eden's successor, Harold Macmillan, campaigning on the slogan 'You've never had it so good' achieved a big Tory majority at the 1959 general election. 'Supermac' and 'Flying Mac', so loved by the cartoonists, was always regarded for his ability by Mason, despite the huge gulf in politics, a good communicator who, despite his aristocratic background, could still appeal to the working man.

Mason's political experience was enhanced through his role as opposition spokesperson on defence and post office affairs. The Labour defence team was headed by the enigmatic George Brown who, despite growing personal problems, Mason regarded as 'a straight man, friendly with most MPs, a good speaker', and 'very able' even a potential prime minister.

Opportunities and appearances apart, the Fifties were certainly difficult years for Labour. The Party, particularly the PLP (Parliamentary Labour Party), was split between Left and Right factions or Bevanites and Gaitskellites. It was torn apart. Nye Bevan and his gang were a significant clique. Mason recalls it as a more severe rift than the recent Blair/Brown situation, opposing members not even talking to each other. Party conferences were often acrimonious affairs. Mason, regarded as an active and energetic young MP, was called upon to address fringe meetings. Yet it was under Gaitskell that Bevan became shadow foreign secretary and, shortly before his death in 1960, deputy leader. Bevan gone, in 1961 Gaitskell was still unable to persuade the Party conference to remove Clause 4 and therefore move towards becoming '...a party of the future, not of the past...' The sudden death of Gaitskell in January 1963 was a great personal blow to Mason who saw him as his mentor, someone he admired and trusted, a family friend - and a prime minister in waiting.

LEY CHRONICLE

South Yorkshire News

and incorporating the "Barnsley Independent"

A.B.C. CERTIFIED NET SALES, JUNE 30, 1952—39,234 COPIES WEEKLY

THREEPENCE

Postage: Three Halfpence

SATURDAY

JANUARY 10, 1953

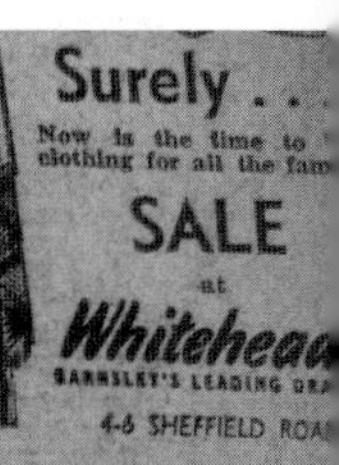

ARTIES AWAIT TALKS WITH M

Resignation rumour: no meetings yet

POKESMAN of Barnsley Conservative and National
Liberal Association told the Barnsley Chronicle yester-
Thursday) that steps had been taken to bring local
election machinery up-to-date following rumours in
wn that the present Socialist M.P. for Barnsley, Mr.
Schofield, was contemplating resigning his seat by
ng for the Stewardship of the Chiltern Hundreds.
The Barnsley Conservative and National Liberal
ientary machine has been set in motion and heads
rtments are beginning to mobilise their forces for
cipated local by-election," the spokesman declared.

behalf of the Barnsley Parliamentary Division Labour
Ald. A. E. McVie, Party secretary, told the Barnsley
e that no official statement would be issued on the local
—"on which there had been so much rumour"—until
ek.

re that announcement was made a full investigation
he facts of the case would be made.

McVie agreed that at the present time Mr. Schofield
ergoing great mental stress following the tragic

Mr. S. Schofield, M.P.

Mr. Geoffrey Whitaker

War victim honoured for fine charity work

SCHOOLS CRIS W.R. CHALLEN

WORSBRO' Grouped Body of Managers of C
Schools decided at a meeting this week t
forward a resolution to pass the school accommo
in Worsbro' on to the County Council.

When the resolution was submitted to the Staincross Divisional Executive Committee last month, a proposal that it be referred back to the Managers pending a visit to Worsbro' by officials of the County Education Committee to discuss education problems in the area, was accepted by representatives of the Worsbro' Managers.

Since the meeting of the Executive Committee, however, the proposed visit by the County Education Committee chairman had been cancelled because he was unable to obtain a County car to make the journey to Worsbro'.

DEATH ARCH

A well know
and surveyor
member of the
goers' Society,
Alfred Whitham
Born in Barn
ham was educ
Grammar Scho
articled to th
Hinchcliffe, arc
veyor. For
practised as a
surveyor in B

Rumour abounded about the future of Barnsley's new Labour MP Sydney Schofield and the possibility of yet another by-election during the opening weeks of 1953, as can be seen in this headline taken from the Barnsley Chronicle of 10 January. The speculation proved to be correct, Schofield, just 42, resigned eleven days later through the Stewardship of the Chiltern Hundreds. An NUM-sponsored MP, he had been elected little more than a year earlier, on 8 November 1951, at a special by-election following the sudden death of Frank Collindridge during the October general election campaign. Later, Schofield revived his political career, becoming a leading figure in the Yorkshire and national miners' union, serving as General Secretary and National Secretary respectively. (Barnsley Chronicle)

Speculation continued in the local press oncerning the scheduling of the by-election and as to whether the Liberal Party would put orward a candidate to make it a three-cornered contest. In the event it was a straight fight between Labour and Conservative. Three front-runners for the Labour nomination emerged: Alderman A E McVie, seen here in this 1960s photograph, Councillor Harry Dancer and the youngest by far, mineworker Roy Mason, of Carlton, already the prospective Labour ndidate for Bridlington but not precluded from consideration for the Barnsley vacancy. McVie was an experienced politician and Secretary of ne Barnsley Labour Party Division and went on become Mayor, in 1954. Dancer also continued to be a high profile local politician, serving as Mayor from 1962-63. (BEC)

MR. MACHEN TO LEAD MINERS

BY a "landslide" victory in the polling for the election to the highest office in the Yorkshire area of the National Union of Mineworkers, Mr. J. K. Alwyn Machen, has this week been elected to fill the office of president of the Yorkshire Area in succession to Mr. J. A. Hall, who retired recently.

In an announcement follow-ng his election, Mr. Machen aid: "I pledge myself and ledicate myself to sustain and o improve the status of the nineworker in Yorkshire."

Voting results, announced at a meeting of the Area Council his week, revealed that Mr. Machen polled 33,669, over 7,000 more than his nearest ival.

The ballot for the presidency vas on the transferable vote ystem, the votes being counted y the Proportional Representa-ion Society. Before the final ount the number of candidates ad been reduced from 10 to hree.

Figures for the final count vere: Mr. Machen, 33,669; Mr. . T. Collins (secretary of Denaby branch N.U.M.), 15,926;

The first step for Mason was to get the Yorkshire miners' nomination for Barnsley. Following a short presentation and questions in the Miners' Hall he was a convincing winner at the selection conference, getting 24 votes, 20 more than the second candidate. An attempt by Jack Wood, an official from Wharncliffe Woodmoor 1,2 & 3 colliery (and subsequently a supporter of Mason) to scupper the proceedings was ruled out of order by Alwyn Machin, seen here, the new and popular president of the Yorkshire area of the NUM. (Barnsley Chronicle)

MR. ROY MASON

MR. GEOFFREY WHITAKER

TWO YOUNG MEN TO DO BATTLE

WHEN Barnsley electors go to the polls in the Barnsley by-election—expected to be sometime in March—they will have a straight choice between two of the youngest Party candidates ever to be put forward in the Barnsley Parliamentary Division. Both candidates are under 30 years of age.

The Barnsley Divisional Labour Party announced their choice of candidate at an adoption conference of all affiliated organisations held in the Miners' Hall, Barnsley, on Monday.

Carrying the Labour mandate

"OTHER END OF THE CAMERA"

Barnsley Chronicle photographer John Geoffrey Richards was at the "other end of the camera" last week,

At a packed Divisional Labour Party conference Mason was chosen as their candidate, casting aside any lingering doubts (given the Schofield resignation) about the wisdom of selecting a miner-sponsored MP, obtaining 148 of the 272 delegate votes, 24 ahead of McVie. 'The rest of the meeting', recalled Roy, 'blurred into a flurry of congratulations, backslapping, commiserations to my opponent, photographs and interviews with the press.' His straight and sincere views prevailed. News soon emerged that the by-election would be contested between two of the youngest candidates ever to stand in the Barnsley Division: Geoffrey Whittaker (Conservative), law student, was 27 and Roy Mason (Labour), miner, 28. At this time an MP under the age of 30 was unusual and NUM-sponsored members were often middle-aged. (Barnsley Chronicle)

hire News
Independent "
–39,408 COPIES WEEKLY

THREEPENCE
Postage: Three Halfpence

SATURDAY
MARCH 21, 1953

NOTABLE SPEAKERS T SUPPORT CANDIDATE

IN an all-out drive to win votes in the forthcoming Barnsley Parliamentary by-election, by the resignation of former Labour M.P., Mr. Sidney Schofield, to be held on T March 31, the Conservative candidate, 27-years-old law student, Mr. Geoffrey Whitak secured the services of prominent personalities in the Conservative Party and the Gover

Mr. Roy Mason

Workless numbers growing

Addressing meetings throughout the constituency this week, the Labour candidate, Mr. Roy Mason, referred to the alarming unemployment figures following the return to power of the Conservatives, and severely criticised the present Government's house allocation policy, and the cuts in the National Health Service, Education, and food subsidies.

Commenting on unemployment, Mr. Mason said that under Labour rule the country had enjoyed 100 per cent. employment, but under Toryism the people had seen for themselves severe unemployment in the textile areas.

"To-day there are over

Among the top line speakers who will support Mr. Whitaker in his election campaign are Dr. Charles Hill, M.P. for Luton, the well-known "Radio Doctor" and now Parliamentary Secretary to the Ministry of Food; the Hon. Richard Wood, M.P. for Bridlington, and the eldest son of Lord Halifax; Mr. D. Heathcoat-Amory, M.P. for Tiverton (Devon); Mr. R. H. Turton, M.C., Parliamentary Secretary to the Ministry of National Insurance; the Rt. Hon. Walter Elliot, M.C., M.P. for Kelvingrove (Glasgow); Mr. W. J. Taylor, C.B.E., M.P. North Bradford; Mr. J. Henderson Stewart, M.P. East Fife; and Mr. Geoffrey Hirst, M.P. Shipley.

Despite the intensified electioneering campaign by the Conservatives, the Labour candidate, 29-years-old miner Mr. Roy Roy Mason, who was the prospective Labour candidate for Bridlington, from which he resigned on being selected Barnsley's candidate, will depend on local speakers throughout his campaign, with the exception of eve-of-poll meetings, when he will have as supporting speakers the Rt. Hon. Alfred Robens, M.P. for Wandsbeck, and former Minister of Labour and Parliamentary Secretary to the Ministry of Fuel and Power; and Mr. R. A. Winterbottom, M.P. for Brightside (Sheffield).

This week, both parties got into full swing and the staffs at the two Committee Rooms were busily completing arrangements for the electioneering work.

Both contesting parties have sent out commando canvassing teams to all parts of the constituency and the two candidates have been busy throughout the week addressing open air meetings on local Council housing estates and making "lightning visits" to local factories and works. In the evenings they have both spoken at two or three meetings at various schools and halls in the Division.

To-night (Friday), Mr. Whitaker will address meetings at Kexborough County Primary School (7 p.m.), Darton Barugh Green School (7.30 p.m.), Higham Church Hall (8 p.m.), and Barnsley Girls' High School (8.15 p.m.). Mr. D. Heathcoat-Amory will be the supporting speaker at the 7.30 and 8.15 p.m. meetings.

Mr. Mason will address two meetings at Darton Modern

Mr. G. Whi

Tories redeem pledg

The most strikin the Barnsley Parli election has been interest shown by the Division. Evi was shown on Wed only 13 people atte Mason's election Grove-street Scho were only about 40 spacious Baths Ha address by the candidate, Whitaker.

Mr. Whitaker this week that the Party had prese employment and state, the very th Socialists had ac trying to destroy.

What was the welfare state? he foundation was nation. A wefar

Although Barnsley was a safe Labour seat, Roy Mason recalled fighting the campaign 'as if the fate of the nation depended on it', addressing meetings at schools, factories and pits in town and nearby villages. The Barnsley Chronicle captured the contrasting tactics of the two candidates: Whittaker drafting in well known speakers early, Mason delaying high-profile visits until the eve of polling, preferring to speak himself on major issues such as unemployment, health and education. (Barnsley Chronicle)

...ARNSLEY CHRONICLE

& South Yorkshire News

and incorporating the "Barnsley Independent"

ESTABLISHED 1858

...ephone 3667 (four lines)

...L. XCIV., 5393

...D AT THE GENERAL POST OFFICE FOR ...ION BEYOND THE UNITED KINGDOM

A.B.C. CERTIFIED NET SALES, DEC. 31, 1952—39,408 COPIES WEEKLY

THREEPENCE
Postage: Three Halfpence

SATURDAY
APRIL 4, 1953

ONLY 58 PER CENT VOTED AT ELECTIO...

MR. GEOFFREY WHITAKER, Conservative candidate in the Barnsley by-election, congratulating his winning opponent, Mr. Roy Mason, the Labour candidate. Also in the picture are the Mayor and Mayoress and the Town Clerk (Mr. A. E. Gilfillan, O.B.E.). (2086)

PIT TO CELEBRATE ITS CENTENARY

WHARNCLIFFE Silkstone Colliery is 100 years old to-day. A marginal note in an old almanack records that Abel Jubb, of Birdwell, was present at the cutting of the first sod on Good Friday, 1853, in the Great Lea field, Tankersley.

Throughout is long career, Wharncliffe Silkstone has given a lead to the South Yorkshire mining industry by pioneer experiments in mining equipment and methods. The most notable figure in its long history was Mr. George Blake Walker, an eminent mining engineer and past president of the Association of Mining Engineers. During his regime the colliery were pioneers in the installation of compressed airdriven coal cutters, coal washery plant, patent by-product ovens and the use of coke oven gas for gas engines generating electricity.

They were one of the first collieries to introduce the Stephenson safety lamp. The distinction of forming the first mines' rescue station in the country was largely due to the courage and foresight of G. B. Walker, who carried out experiments at Wharncliffe Silkstone long before the rescue station ... well Station to a point in close proximity to the colliery.

The original intention was to build the station adjacent to the main road near the Rescue Station at Birdwell.

The colliery was opened in 1854 during a period of depression and its early years were marked by a series of strikes and lock-outs, culminating in the formation of the first miners' union in 1858. This was organised by a Wharncliffe Silkstone collier, John Normansell, who later became first secretary of the South Yorkshire Miners' Association, forerunner of the N.U.M.

The eviction of Normansell from his position of checkweighman by the owners of Wharncliffe Silkstone resulted in a Royal Commission being appointed in 1868 to enquire into the organisation and rules of Trades Unionism. As a result, a clause was inserted in ...

...ry, the ...repre... Mary's (2070)

MINER'S HEAD TRAPPED BY FALL OF COAL

A SEARCHING inquiry into the use of "pinch-bars"—an instrument used for pulling coal from the face—was conducted at an inquest at Hoyland on Monday on an Elsecar ...

Labour holds seat

IN one of the quietest local election campaigns within re... years the Socialist candidate, Mr. Roy Mason, of Ca... was returned as M.P. for the Barnsley Parliamentary Div... when he polled a total of 18,378 votes over his Conserv... opponent, Mr. Geoffrey Whitaker.

Nearly half of the electorate of the Division fail... exercise their vote in a campaign marked for its general ... of interest. The percentage of poll was only 58 per ce...

Chief interest in the outcome of the election was centred on the question whether the Conservative candidate, in his second attempt, could reduce the majority obtained by Socialist candidates in previous campaigns.

On the reduced poll of 40,188 the Conservative candidate gained 1,609 votes over his 1951 General Election figure of 9,296. The Socialist candidate polled 8,240 votes less than the figure cast for the previous Socialist candidate. On the last occasion, when there was a Liberal candidate in the field some 7,000 votes were cast in favour of the Liberal.

The Labour majority was reduced on this occasion from 28,227 to 18,378.

Result: Mr. Roy Mason (Soc.) 29,283; Mr. Geoffrey Whitaker (Con.), 10,905.

First ballot box was received at the Public Hall at 9.9 p.m. from the St. John's School polling station and the last of the boxes was returned at 9.30 p.m. from the Wesleyan Reform S.S. at Mapplewell.

In the presence of an unusually small crowd the result was finally declared at 11.10 p.m.

Mr. H. R. Crow

DEATH O... A FORME... SALESMA...

A well-known Bas... man in the coal sales...

Tuesday 31 March 1953 was polling day, a few days after the death of Queen Mary. Although the turn out was perhaps understandably low, just 58 per cent, Mason still got 18,378 votes more than Whittaker. Shouts of 'Good old Roy' were heard from the direction of the gallery in the Public Hall when the results were announced and a lone voice sang the first few words of the Red Flag as the election party departed from the Hall. (Barnsley Chronicle)

Another photograph with Mr and Mrs Horace Holmes on the terrace at Westminster on the day of Roy Mason's introduction to the House, 14 April 1953. Looking smart, Mason's suit was in fact the same one that he wore at his marriage eight years earlier! A yard-by-yard rehearsal took place the day before, but when it came to making the oath he had to shout over the noise from chatting members, a not unusual occurrence. (MA)

This rare photograph shows some of the leading political figures of Barnsley in the early 1950s. Roy Mason (note the bow-tie) and his wife Marjorie are at a presentation of gifts in Carlton Working Men's Club to the new Mayor and Mayoress of Barnsley, Councillor Lawrence Briggs and Ada Hill (his sister-in-law). Lawrence Briggs' mayoralty (1952-53) included Roy Mason's early weeks at Westminster. Briggs was succeeded by George Burkinshaw (standing, first right) and the previous Mayor of Barnsley, Richard Newman (third right, wearing glasses) was also in attendance. Richard's grandson is the present Barnsley Councillor William 'Bill' Newman who was Mayor from 2003-4. The lady presenting the gifts, Gwen Bright, served as Mayor from 1978-79 when Roy Mason was Secretary of State for Northern Ireland. (MA)

The early months spent living in London were financially difficult for the young Barnsley MP and for his family at home, having spent seven weeks canvassing with no wages and living in the capital for a week before receiving any parliamentary pay. A settling-in gift of £50 from his father-in-law, Ernest Sowden, seen here with Roy and mother-in-law Minnie on an early visit to the Commons, was a lifeline. Mason stayed at the West Central Hotel in Southampton Row, along with several other coalfield MPs, where bed and breakfast was cheap: 16s.6d [c.80p]. On this photograph, dating from about 1954, the old wedding suit appears to have been replaced. Note the pipe which was to become such a familiar item. (MA)

Pointing towards the Thames, Commons terrace photograph showing Mason with a group of constituency supporters, probably miners from his home village of Carlton. (MA)

Clement Attlee was elected to Parliament in 1922, becoming Labour leader in 1935 (until 1955, an exceptional period) and Prime Minister from 1945-51. Attlee, aged 70 in 1953, was a legendary figure, so when his PPS (Parliamentary Private Secretary), Arthur Moyles, summoned novice MP Roy Mason to his office a few days following the latter's introduction to the House he went there, as we have seen, with some trepidation. Mason had to approach him 'like a schoolboy'. Tom Williams, the veteran miner-MP from the Don Valley constituency was sited as an exemplar for him. Then a quick 'Thank you' concluded a brief meeting.' (MA)

The two senior Labour MPs who helped young Mason find his feet in the Commons were Tom Williams and Wilfred Paling. This 1950s photograph, taken outside the House, shows a group of Labour MPs and miners' leaders welcoming two foreign guests. Tom Williams can be seen just to the left of Mason (and 5th from the left of the group); and Wilfred Paling is the second person on Mason's left, standing next to Albert Roberts MP who is on the extreme right. Roy recalls Williams as 'a wonderful man, straight as a ramrod, with white curly hair and always wearing wing collars and bow-tie. He suffered from arthritis and I would get him his coffee in a morning. We became friends. On one occasion the young Queen was concerned about his welfare as he was missing from Ascot. Tom was a great horseracing man.' Paling was the member for Dearne Valley and had the largest majority (35, 410) of any MP at the 1945 general election. (MA)

Mr. Roy Mason (Barnsley): I rise with some trepidation, having been a Member of this House for a very short time, to make my first speech. I ask for the indulgence of the House on this occasion and shall do my utmost to observe the custom and practice that has developed in this House, firstly of being brief and, secondly, of being non-controversial. The first may prove easy, but the second may prove more difficult.

On the passing of the Bill—as I see it as a Member representing an industrial constituency with the feelings of his constituents at heart, and not as an economist—we shall witness once more the redistribution of wealth from those who are least able to afford it to those who least require it. I can foresee that after this Budget, as I saw after the last one, we shall witness once more the cleavage between the poor and the rich made more distinct. We shall see the wealthy made more wealthy and we shall see members of the lower income groups made relatively worse off.

During our term of office we distributed the wealth of the nation substantially and effectively in a more equitable manner, but with each succeeding Tory Budget we shall see the restoration back to the previous level of the wage incomes prior to 1939 when we had successive Tory Governments. For instance, fairly recently we have seen two different types of bread produced. Because the Government realise that there are two distinct classes, we are producing one type of bread for the worse off and another for those who can afford a higher quality. We witnessed that in the case of margarine and butter prior to 1939, when the relatively worse off could not afford to buy the best butter available for those with large purses.

The Chancellor said this was an incentive Budget, an incentive to produce more this coming year. I ask the Chancellor this question: Is it an incentive to my constituents since my constituency is predominantly coalmining? Is it an incentive to the surface workers, to the underground on-cost workers who are below the Income Tax level and cannot benefit by the Income Tax reductions? Is it not also noticeable to these lower paid workers that the percentage reduction of Purchase Tax is less on the commodities that come within the orbit of the working-class purse? Quite respectfully, I say that the Budget has been no incentive whatever to those people to work harder and to produce more.

Roy Mason made his maiden speech (shown in part here) in the Commons on the afternoon of Thursday 7 May 1953, favouring Tom Williams' advice of being honest, brief and to the point - but well prepared (rather than a more spontaneous approached suggested by Paling). This extract is from Hansard, the official record of parliament. The speech lasted 8 minutes and was well received. Mason was immediately congratulated by the member for Ayr, Sir Thomas Moore, who made the comment that the young MP 'obviously feels very deeply about the matters of which he spoke, and...showed a complete knowledge of the subjects he discussed'. The Chancellor of the Exchequer, R A Butler added his congratulations, as did a former Labour Chancellor and soon-to-be Labour leader and friend, Hugh Gaitskell, who referred to his speech as 'brief, fluent, firm and clear - four excellent qualities - and we look forward to hearing from him again in the near future'. (Hansard/MA)

A few days after making his maiden speech, on 20 May 1953, Mason made a useful contribution to the Finance Bill when a debate on the new Entertainment Duty was discussed. He referred to the plight of his recently relegated home team, Barnsley Football Club who had been obliged to sell key players because of poor attendance at home fixtures as they had been forced to increase admission charges because of increased taxation. He cited the most regrettable sale as that of Tommy Taylor for about £30,000 to Manchester United. Taylor soon became an international of great promise but was one of the Busby Babes killed in the Munich Air Disaster of 6 February 1958. (Peter Taylor, Barnsley Memories Magazine)

Winston Churchill was in his final premiership (1951-55) during Roy Mason's early years as an MP. Their first 'meeting' was memorable. Mason was floored when the great man accidentally caught him with his shoulder when they were both on their way to the Division Lobby at the end of a late night debate. Young Mason, still wearing his precious wedding suit, was helped to his feet and brushed down by the great man who continued his business without saying a word. (MA)

BARNSLEY CHRONICL

ESTABLISHED 1858

Telephone 3667 (four lines)

VOL. XCVI., 5495

REGISTERED AT THE GENERAL POST OFFICE FOR TRANSMISSION BEYOND THE UNITED KINGDOM

& South Yorkshire News

and incorporating the " Barnsley Independent "

A.B.C. CERTIFIED NET SALES, DEC. 31, 1954, 40,729 COPIES WEEKLY

THREEPEN

Postage : Twop

SATURDA

MARCH 19,

FIVE EDITIONS COVERING TOWN, WOMBWELL, HOYLAND, PENISTONE, CUDWORTH, ROYSTON AND GRIMETHORPE.

BARNSLEY M.P. CRITICISES PREMIER ON THE H-BOMB

NEW-BORN LAMBS are always a sign that Spring is just around the corner, and during the recent spell of sunny weather our photographer visited Swithan Farm at Haigh to meet "Jimmy," an orphan lamb, who is being cared for by Marian Chapman, of Kexbro', seen here (right) with a friend, Anne Harding of Barnsley. (4738)

THE BOMB! The Barnsley Member of Parliament, Mr. Roy Mason, made an important contribution in the House of Commons debate this week on world disarmament in which he called for an immediate meeting of the world powers with a view to stopping all further atomic and hydrogen explosions. Mr. Mason, who spoke for 15 minutes, had the privilege of following the Prime Minister in the debate, and was the first Labour back-bencher to take part in the debate.

MR. W. T. J. STEAD, of 90, Huddersfield-road, Barnsley, photogrpahed outside Buckingham Palace with his wife and son, Phillip J. Stead, the author, when he received the M.B.E. this week.

Festival in May planned

Plans are going ahead for the annual competitive music festival at Barnsley on May 14, and it is expected to be the most ambitious programme than in any previous year.

For the first time there will be a prize in nearly all 45

After Mr. Mason had finished speaking on the dangers of atmospheric radiation as his plea for the banning of the bomb tests, a Conservative member described his speech as "hair raising—but no doubt accurate."

"Unless these experiments cease, the radiation in the atmosphere will be so great that we shall be unable to control it. It will then be too late," he said.

Mr. Mason pleaded: "In view of these hidden dangers to all mankind, I think it is the duty of the Prime Minister and of the Foreign Secretary to call an immediate meeting of the Powers concerned with a view to stopping all further

Mr. Roy Mason, M.P.

As yet no person or conveyance, on land, sea or in the air can escape the effects of a thermo-nuclear war.

"Ships in the vicinity of an under water thermo-nuclear explosion would be like matchsticks in an erupting volcano. Concentrations of armies could be blasted out of existence, and cities picked off the surface of the earth like dead flies off a flypaper."

He continued: "However, I do not think that the explosion is the worst feature of the hydrogen bomb. Undoubtedly, the worst feature is radioactivity in its various and unlimited forms.

"To find a defence against this we are still delving into an unknown and little ventured

Elected to Co-op. Guild executive

The 450 members of the Barns ley Guild of Co-operators pres ent at their meeting this wee applauded the announceme that their president, Mrs. S. Thompson, had been elected the executive of the Nation Guild of Co-operators as Nor Eastern section representati for a period of two years.

Congratulations to M Thompson were added by Co Mrs. M. Brannan, speaking behalf of members of Barns

Mason's second encounter with Churchill took place in a packed chamber following the discovery that the government intended to develop the hydrogen bomb, a revelation which caused great consternation from the Labour Party at a time when there was a growing anti-nuclear and 'Ban the Bomb' lobby. Mason was called to speak just after Churchill had finished his typically impressive oration by which time there was a great exodus of members, so his moment to impress was little heard and the government easily overcame the censure motion. Nevertheless, the young MP's efforts did manage to grab the headlines in his hometown press, published on 19 March 1955. (Barnsley Chronicle)

As time progressed, young Mason became more confident in Commons debates, making valuable contributions on matters relevant to his home constituency as well as (taking Attlee's advice to specialise) defence. One of his early campaigns - despite the teatime teasing of some parliamentary colleagues - concerned the great pit spoil heaps or muckstacks that dominated the old coalfield areas of Britain. Harold Macmillan, the Minister responsible, published a Spoil Heaps circular, local authorities had to check their muckstacks and scenes like this one, of Mason's old pit heap at Carlton, would gradually disappear under a succession of land reclamation schemes. (Chris and Pearl Sharp/Old Barnsley)

Sir Anthony Eden became prime minister following the resignation of Sir Winston Churchill on 5 April 1955 and an election was called for 26 May. It was therefore back on the campaign trail for Roy Mason, for the first time in a general election. The outcome was another defeat for the Labour Party but Mason, still only 31, was returned with an increased majority of over 24,000 votes. (Roy Sabine)

REGISTERED AT THE GENERAL POST OFFICE FOR TRANSMISSION BEYOND THE UNITED KINGDOM

and incorporating the "Barnsley Independent"

A.B.C. CERTIFIED NET SALES, JUNE 30, 1955, 41,654 COPIES WEEKLY

FIVE EDITIONS COVERING TOWN, WOMBWELL, HOYLAND, PENISTONE, CUDWORTH, ROYSTON AND GR

LEADS WITH BOSSES TO EM

139 people are crying out for jobs

IT is in the hands of the leaders of Barnsley's industrial and commercial undertakings to alleviate the plight of 139 local men and women who cry out for work. Yesterday (Thursday) the Barnsley M.P., Mr. Roy Mason, issued an appeal to all employers in Barnsley to find work for these 139 people who are disabled—and daily growing more dispirited.

The problem can be solved with the co-operation of employers, Mr. Mason declared. It would only mean each firm with a payroll of over 20 employees in the town taking an additional employee on the staff.

In Barnsley there are 139 unemployed disabled persons. In Barnsley there are 164 firms employing more than 20 workers. The register of unemployed could be reduced to nil overnight.

In issuing his appeal to Barnsley employers, Mr. Mason speaks on behalf of the disabled. It was two spokesmen for the disabled who contacted Mr. Mason during his Advice Bureau session at the Town Hall. They said they had "reached the end of their tether."

"What does the future hold for us?" asked the two men. "Here we have a boom period in Barnsley and cannot find work. What will happen in the future? What future have we to look forward to?"

Mr. Mason promised to help in whatever way he could these men and their disabled that the phrases used by the Exchange staff are not just empty pious remarks. At one time in this area there were over 1,000 men and women who were regarded as a hard core of unemployment as far as industry was concerned.

During the last nine to 12 months this figure has been worked down until at the present time there are 104 men and 35 women without employment due to disabilities which range from ulcerated stomachs, general debility to amputations. There are four cases where the disablement is so severe that only sheltered employment is the answer; at one time there were 19 such cases.

Total number on the Barnsley Exchange disabled persons register is 2,340—2,124 men and 216 women. During the last 12 months 512 men and women have been placed in employment.

Of the present unemployed total of 139, 15 are under 40 years of age, 44 aged between 40 and 50; and the largest group, 80 cases over 50 years.

SUCCESS STORY

Guard of honour by Cadets

When the long awaited film, "The Dam Busters" is screened at the Ritz Cinema, Barnsley, in the near future, a guard of honour will be provided by the members of the Barnsley 148 Squadron of the Air Training Corps.

On Monday, October 3, the Mayor of Barnsley, Coun. J. H. Foster, will visit the Ritz to inspect the guard of honour, and will later present a special trophy which is being awarded in conjunction with the film to a member of the Squadron.

"The Dambuster Trophy" will go to the most outstanding Cadet of the Barnsley Battn., and will be awarded annually.

The film will be heralded by a special fanfare of bugles, played by A.T.C. members. The

MR. R.

POLIO V
RYHILL'S

EVERYONE at Ryhil Mr. Richard Eastw

Mason treated his constituency work very seriously, giving a fair allocation of his weekend time to both town and borough. The latter involved mobile, informal surgeries 'on the hoof' and in places such as clubs and pubs. It was a pattern that became well known and certainly helped with his popularity at elections. People with disabilities were also included, visited in their homes within a few days of any request. Shortly after the election he campaigned for work to be found for unemployed disabled people, as can be seen in this headline from the town newspaper which appeared on 24 September. (Barnsley Chronicle)

Roy with wife Marjorie and daughter Susan at the baptism of Jill Diane in the Crypt Chapel of the House of Commons on 22 July 1955. Jill was born on 4 March. The godparents were the Labour MPs Harriet Slater and Hugh Gaitskell (MA)

Another local issue which resulted in an intense campaign at Westminster was the question of inadequate hospital provision for Barnsley. The Tory Minister of Health, Enoch Powell (seen here, left of the Matron, with Mason on her right on a visit to Mount Vernon Hospital, Barnsley, in 1961), wilted under a barrage of 30 parliamentary questions from Mason in just three weeks, so much so that in the tearoom queue he asked the Barnsley MP to see him in his office. The outcome was an assurance that a new Barnsley Hospital was now at the top of the priority list and would stay there 'short of war!' The Government allocated finance for the new Barnsley District General Hospital in 1961 and the foundation stone laid six years later. (MA)

Clem Attlee resigned his leadership of the Labour Party shortly after the 1955 election defeat and was replaced by a much younger man, Hugh Gaitskell, Mason's mentor and valued friend. Here Gaitskell is speaking at a Yorkshire Miners' Gala. Roy Mason is seated in the background, partly obscured by the Mayor. Miners' President Sam Bullough is seated to the left of Gaitskell. (MA)

Mason, looking smart in blazer and slacks, at a 1950s Labour Party conference in Blackpool, with colleagues Alice Cullen and Cyril Bence. This was a time of considerable infighting with the Left becoming more vociferous under Aneurin Bevan. Bence was MP for the Scottish constituency of East Dunbartonshire. Cullen represented Glasgow Gorbels and was the first Roman Catholic woman MP. Mason was a close friend of Bence during his early years in parliament, remembering him with affection as 'a grand and earnest politician'. (MA)

In a marquee at another 1950s Labour Party conference, Cyril Bence to Mason's right. Also present are Harold Simms, the Party's regional organiser and his wife, Mary. At this time Mason was invited to speak at fringe meetings but he recalled party conferences as being 'miserable for those of us who wanted to concentrate on fighting the Tories'. (MA)

Marjorie Mason with daughters Susan and Jill at their home, now 1 Victoria Street, central Barnsley, where they had moved in the late 1950s. A large rented house, quite a change from the small Carlton prefab. (MA)

The Masons at home in the late 1950s. This image by local photographers Denton's was used for the family's Christmas card. (Denton & Co Ltd)

In 1956 Roy Mason was part of a parliamentary delegation to the Gold Coast on the eve of its independence just before it was renamed Ghana. He rightly became suspicious of its prime minister, Kwame Nkrumah, who continued in office (as President from 1960) until being overthrown in the coup of 1966. Nkrumah created a single party state aligned more to the Soviet Union than the West. During the debate on the Bill of Independence Mason had warned the House that hopes for the new African country would be disappointing. (MA)

Frank Goodwin and Roy Mason MP meeting local dignitaries in Brong/Ahafo or Ashanti, Gold Coast. (Mike Patteson/MA)

With Frank Goodwin from the Chief Commissioner's office and a local chief, Gold Coast. (Mike Patteson MC/MA)

Aneurin ('Nye') Bevan was a key figure of the Left, described by Mason as 'a giant of a character, eloquent, passionate and full of fire' but Mason did not like his fellow former miner's politics which he felt made Labour increasingly unelectable, voting to have the whip withdrawn. A shocked Bevan told Mason that he would 'never forgive' him, brandishing a large fist in his face. (BEC)

At the October 1959 general election the predicted confidence in Roy Mason being returned for a third time proved to be correct. Standing against Buckinghamshire solicitor Howard Bent, the Tory candidate, Mason's majority was increased to 27, 376 (cf 18,378 in 1955). However, 'Supermac's' (Harold Macmillan's) Conservatives under his 'You've never had it so good' slogan inflicted a crashing defeat on Labour in the country as a whole. (Barnsley Chronicle)

THE GENERAL ELECTION

MEET THE CANDIDATES

CONFIDENT MR. MASON

Barnsley Divisional Labour Party are confident that their candidate, Mr. Roy Mason, will be returned to Parliament for the third time with an increased majority.

At the 1955 election, Mr. Mason had a 24,709 majority over his Conservative opponent. He was first returned to Parliament in a by-election in 1953 when his majority was 18,378.

Mr. Mason (36), was born at Royston, and worked as an underground fitter at Wharncliffe Woodmoor Colliery. He was delegate from the Colliery Union branch to the Yorkshire Council of the N.U.M., and before being adopted as the miners' nominee for election to the House of Commons was prospective Labour candidate for Bridlington.

During his six years in the House Mr. Mason has taken an active part in many debates and has strengthened his contributions by taking part in many "fact finding" missions.

Married, with two children—Susan and Jill—he has his campaign headquarters at the Miners' Hall, Barnsley, where he will be holding his eve-of-poll meeting.

He can be heard speaking to-night (Friday) at Wilthorpe Junior School, on Sunday morning at Ardsley, on Monday at the Edward Sheerien School, Athersley, on Tuesday at Brook Motors, Barugh Green, and eve-of-poll meetings at Bank End Hall, Worsbrough Dale, Kexborough, and the Miners' Hall, Barnsley.

DETERMINED MR. BENT

Barnsley Conservative candidate for election to the House of Commons is Mr. John Phillip Howard Bent, a 49-years-old company director, of Beaconsfield, Bucks., who has spent 20 years in India as managing director of a tea company.

Educated at Harrow and Cambridge, Mr. Bent was managing director of Jardine Henderson Ltd., of Calcutta, India and controlled two collieries, six Jute mills and 30 tea factories.

He was chairman of the Indian Tea Association in 1956-57, and in 1956 was a member of a delegation appointed by the Indian Government to visit America to investigate publicity work of tea councils in the States and Canada.

Since his return to this country he has been an active member of the Penn (Bucks.) Conservative Association and a member of the Branch Committee. He is married with one daughter.

During the election campaign he is concentrating on

meeting the voters pe ally and to-morrow (S day) will again be avai for questioning at the servative stall on Ma hill.

He continues his gramme of public mee to-night (Friday) at Barnsley Grammar Sc followed by meetings Monday (St. Matt School) and Tuesday (Bretton Church Hall).

His eve-of-poll me will be at the Barnsley School for Girls.

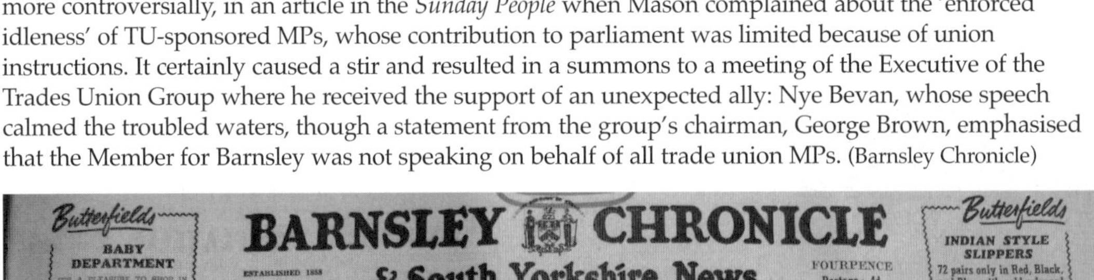

Making a name for himself in constituency and parliament also had occasional criticism within his own party. For example, saying that DJs were guilty of 'song-plugging' (even though it was certainly true!). Or, more controversially, in an article in the *Sunday People* when Mason complained about the 'enforced idleness' of TU-sponsored MPs, whose contribution to parliament was limited because of union instructions. It certainly caused a stir and resulted in a summons to a meeting of the Executive of the Trades Union Group where he received the support of an unexpected ally: Nye Bevan, whose speech calmed the troubled waters, though a statement from the group's chairman, George Brown, emphasised that the Member for Barnsley was not speaking on behalf of all trade union MPs. (Barnsley Chronicle)

BARNSLEY CHRONICLE
& South Yorkshire News

ESTABLISHED 1858 | VOL. C., 5733 | and incorporating the "Barnsley Independent" | FOURPENCE Postage: 4d. | SATURDAY, NOVEMBER 28, 1959

A.B.C. CERTIFIED NET SALES, DEC. 31, 1958, 41,221 COPIES WEEKLY

FIVE EDITIONS COVERING TOWN, WOMBWELL, HOYLAND, PENISTONE, CUDWORTH, ROYSTON AND GRIMETHORPE

BARNSLEY MP AND HIS RELATIONS WITH UNIONS

RESENTMENT OVER ARTICLE AMONG LABOUR MEMBERS

NATIONAL Press publicity which has been given to an article by the Barnsley M.P., Mr. R. Mason, has earned for him a vote of censure. His trade union colleagues in the House of Commons told him this week that the contents of his article were "inaccurate" and that he had no right to claim that he was speaking for nearly 100 Labour M.Ps.

And this was the second time this week that Mr. R. Mason had been told that he does not know what he is talking about. The second occasion was when he alleged that "disc jockeys" were guilty of song-plugging.

The article which gave rise to the censure move was published in a Sunday newspaper. It was headlined: "Labour's Crisis" and by the side of a photograph of Mr. Mason, it announced: "I speak for 100 gagged men."

On seeing the article—which was critical of the manner in which trade union M.P.s are allegedly prevented from asking questions on industrial issues in the House—the trade union members immediately protested.

The terms of the article aroused so much resentment among the Labour members in the trade union group—and Mr. Mason is himself a Miners' Union nominee—that they demanded that he should be asked to explain his article.

NO DOUBT

The result of the storm of protest was that Mr. Mason was called before the Executive of the Trades Union Group in the House of Com-

MR. H. A. REDBURN

HONOUR FOR THE TOWN

Mr. H. A. Redburn, Director of Education, has accepted an invitation to serve on the Admiralty Interview Board for the selection of candidates for the award of Royal Naval Scholarships tenable at the Royal Naval College, Dartmouth.

The Board will sit at H.M.S. ...an, Gosport, for approximately four weeks beginning on ...uary 9, 1960.

Congratulating Mr. Redburn on his appointment, Ald. A. E. ...s, chairman of the Education Committee, at its meeting Monday, pointed out that the ... offered to Mr. Redburn ... been the only one for a

PLAN FOR VILLAGE HALL

Plans for the building of a village hall for Mapplewell and Staincross are to be discussed at a special meeting called for December 4, to which representatives of all the local organisations have been invited.

Sponsors of the idea have already made inquiries into the possibility of financial help from the County authorities, and it is felt that the enterprise would stand a good chance of success if the whole village gave its backing.

Coun. Vernon Ledger told the Barnsley Chronicle that he and several other interested persons had looked round a hall built in the Rotherham area and had decided that a similar community centre would be ideal for Mapplewell.

"It could be used for whist drives, dances, meetings, and so on," he said, "and it would also be an ideal place for pensioners to spend some of their leisure time.

THEIR OWN

"We are particularly interested in old people. They don't all want to go into public houses on social occasions, for example, and it is felt that they would be far more comfortable in a place of this sort.

"I think it would also appeal to the younger ones. It would be a building that we could really call our own. We've seen a similar venture which has proved a success, and we

TREVOR WILLETTS

TREVOR ON AIR AGAIN

Well-known local organist, Mr. Trevor Willetts, is to make his ninth broadcast this year when next Friday he gives a recital from the organ of the Ritz Cinema, Barnsley.

The recital, one of three recorded at the cinema on November 2, will be broadcast at 6.50 p.m. in the Northern Home Service and will last for 10 minutes. The two other recitals will be broadcast at later dates.

The programme will include "Dixie Ragbag," "Tango Ecstasy" and "Cockney Polka."

Mr. Willetts learned to play the organ at the age of four and played in many local churches

WATER POSITION STILL CRITICAL

DESPITE warnings about the danger of reverting to normal water consumption, the economy practised in Barnsley during the dry weather has not been continued, and the position is serious.

There are only 42 days' supply of water left, and there can be no resting of all the bore-holes which is vital at this stage if grave trouble is to be avoided next summer.

Mr. W. Gordon Lees, Barnsley's Water Engineer, told the Barnsley Chronicle yesterday (Thursday): "Having seen some rain, the consumers think they can now go ahead and use the normal amount of water, but I must again appeal to them not to do so.

"I have every sympathy with them, but I must let them know what the situation is, and it is serious."

On Tuesday morning, he said, despite a slight rise in the reservoirs, a day's supply was lost through increased consumption.

Mr. Lees explained that 1,620 million gallons of water was required in the next 126 to 130 days. "We cannot possibly get that amount if people carry on as they have done in the last week or 10 days," he emphasised.

When full, the reservoirs had

JIM SIMPSON

Bull-fight youth has

EMPLOYEES of the Remploy factory, Barnsley, who submitted entries to the Remploy Art Exhibition, are informed by Mr. T. W. Harrison, manager, that their work has won the Chairman's Cup for the most outstanding entries in the exhibition.

PRINTING FIRM WINDS UP

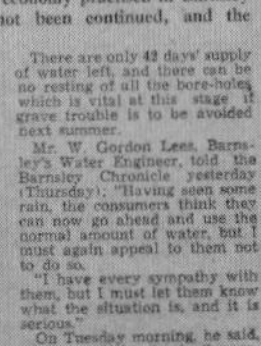

BARNSLEY REMPLO FACTORY WINS CU

A CUP presented this year for the first time to the Remploy factory submitting the most outstanding number of entries to the Remploy art exhibition has been won by the Barnsley factory for disabled persons.

HEATERS F SCHOOLS

Mason's growing knowledge and ability in the Commons resulted in his first responsibility as a Labour spokesman on Post Office matters and a junior member of George Brown's shadow defence team. An early and successful campaign was to ensure that the bodies of armed service personnel killed abroad should be transported home free of charge. Incredibly, the families of soldiers who died on duty in Germany were expected to pay for the costs of flying the coffin of their loved one home to Britain. Shaming the Tories in the Commons over this issue resulted in a change of policy, his relatively recent memories of the lack of respect given to dead pitmen not forgotten. Brown is seen here speaking at the 1967 Yorkshire Miners' Gala held in Barnsley. (BEC)

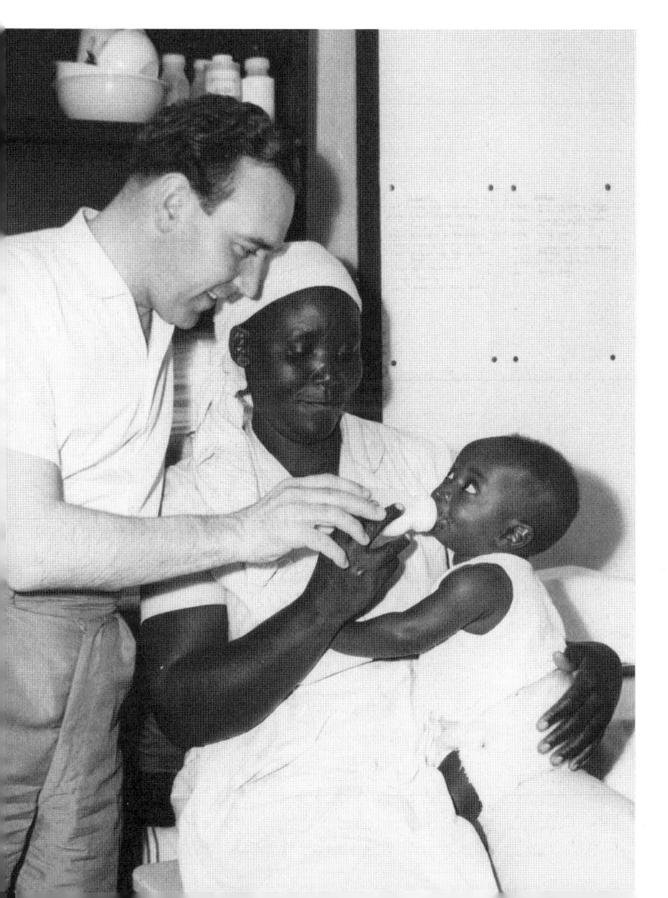

Mason was in Africa again, in 1960, part of a small delegation visiting the new (founded 1953) Federation of Rhodesia and Nyasaland. It was dissolved three years later, Northern Rhodesia becoming part of the independent republic of Zambia, with Kenneth Kaunda as president. Southern Rhodesia's prime minister Ian Smith declared unilateral independence from Britain in 1965. In 1980, as Zimbabwe, it gained full independence under its enigmatic and present leader, Robert Mugabe. This photograph shows Roy Mason at a health centre, S. Rhodesia. (MA)

Roy Mason at a school, S.Rhodesia, 1960. (MA)

More international experience, this time in Europe. Mason was part of a Labour Party / TU delegation visiting Berlin in 1962. Here the group look at the growing Berlin Wall. Roy Mason, pipe in one hand, camera in the other, is second right standing on the bottom of the viewing platform. Almost directly above him, sandwiched between pointing MPs, is Harold Wilson, soon to become Labour leader and prime minister. Other TU-sponsored MPs present include Charles Loughlin (Gloucester West), Joe Slater (Sedgefield), Marcus Lipton (Brixton), Edwin Wainwright (Dearne Valley), Eddie Milne (Blyth), Elfred Davies (Rhondda East), Billy Blyton (Houghton-le-Spring), Sydney Irving (Dartford), Joe Harper (Pontefract & Castleford), Victor Yates (Birmingham Ladywood) and Norman Pentland (Chester-le-Street). (MA)

Labour leader Hugh Gaitskell, seen here with his successor, Harold Wilson, died on 18 January 1963. It was a great blow to Mason, the loss of a mentor and good friend. However, it would be under Wilson's skilful leadership that the politically maturing Mason emerged as a front bench opposition spokesman and a new chapter in his fast-moving life began. (BEC)

Part Four

Minister Mason

The First Wilson Government, 1964-70

'I had to grapple with the everyday realities of ministerial life, learning how to work with two private secretaries, a diary secretary and platoons of advisers...'

Official photograph after Mason's appointment as Minister of State (Shipping) at the Board of Trade in October 1964. The post also included responsibility for Tourism and Travel. (MA)

Life and Times

1964	[16.10]	General Election: Labour win with a majority of only 4 seats and Harold Wilson forms his first Government; Mason retains his Barnsley seat for the third time, polling 37,250 votes (27,833 majority).
	[18.10.]	Mason appointed Minister of State at the Board of Trade with responsibility for Shipping & Tourism.
1965	[Jan]	Mason in Tokyo; instigates a major review of Shipbuilding and introduces important Safety at Sea improvements.
	[22.7]	Sir Alec Douglas Home resigns as Conservative Party leader.
	[28.7]	Edward Heath is new leader of Conservative Party.
1966	[31.3]	General Election: Labour re-elected with a majority of 96; Mason retains his Barnsley seat for the fourth time, polling 38,744 votes (26,288 majority).
	[21.4]	Opening of Parliament televised for the first time.
	[3.5]	Mason visits Moscow, meets Alexey Kosygin in the Kremlin re Gerald Brooke, the jailed British lecturer.
	[16.5]	Seamen's strike begins.
	[21.10]	Aberfan disaster, 144 killed when an old pit heap slips onto a South Wales junior school.
1967	[Jan]	Mason promoted to Minister of State for Defence Equipment (and later Civil Aviation), under Denis Healey.
	[17.1]	Mason in Paris, opening innovatory air traffic control centre. Mason in Tehran, meets the Shah of Persia and obtains lucrative tank export order.
	[19.3]	Oil spillage disaster when *Torrey Canyon* runs aground off Lands End.
	[11.5]	Britain applies to join EEC.
	[17.10]	Mason has supersonic flight in Lightening fighter aircraft.
	[20.10]	On the Clyde: Mason launches HMS *Antrim*, guided missile destroyer. Mason visits Japan and Brazil.
	[10.12]	Mason Receives unaminous vote of confidence by Barnsley Divisional Labour Party following 93-8 defeat of Woolley Colliery NUM branch resolution that he was not fully representating local miners.
1968	[26.1]	Now 'Right Honourable' Roy Mason MP, becomes a member of the Privy Council following a ceremony at Buckingham Palace.
	[Apr]	Mason promoted to Postmaster-General, suceeding Edward 'Ted' Short.
	[2.7]	Mason appointed Minister of Power (and therefore member of the Cabinet), after resignation of Ray Gunter.

1968/69		Mason faces an uneasy role in context of a wave of pit closures and the commissioning of Seaton Carew nuclear power station.
1969	[21.6]	Mason speaks at the Yorkshire Miners' Gala, Barnsley. Opposes Barbara Castle's *In Place of Strife* White Paper on trade union reform.
	[21.7]	American astronaut Neil Armstrong is the first man to walk on the moon. Mason hosts reception for Apollo 11 moon landing astronauts at Downing Street.
	[Oct]	Mason appointed President of the expanded Board of Trade, succeeding Anthony Crosland.
	[Nov+]	Mason's overseas visits include meeting King Hussein of Jordan and Dom Mintoff, the Maltese Labour leader.
	[26.12]	Marriage of Susan Mason (Roy and Marjorie's older daughter) to Allen Duke, St Mary's, Barnsley.
1970	[18.6]	General Election: Conservatives win with a 30-seat majority and Edward Heath becomes Prime Minister; Mason wins his sixth consituency election in Barnsley with 34,956 votes (24,145 majority).

Overview

Although the death of Hugh Gaitskell was a personal and professional blow to Mason, he was soon impressed by the clever and energetic political skills of his successor, Harold Wilson, especially during debates in the Commons against the aristocratic and dull Sir Alec Douglas-Home. The Tories had reeled under the Profumo scandal during 1963, and were perfect fodder for the new satyrical television programme *That Was the Week That Was*. 'We sensed', recalled Mason, 'Labour was winning at last.'

Reference to the index of *Hansard* for the 1962-63 parliamentary session shows that Mason had been very active, speaking and tabling questions on issues such as aviation, defence and the armed forces, energy and a variety of local concerns. He was also able to speak with confidence on international matters: Central Africa and Rhodesia, the Middle East and Europe.

Labour's narrow election victory in October 1964 was the start of an extraordinary successful period for the Barnsley MP, ascending from the role of opposition spokesperson to junior minister, and onwards to become a respected senior politician of cabinet rank, five notable appointments in six years. 'Feeling elated', Lord Mason remembered, 'after each appointment'. Wilson clearly recognised some aspects of his own character and political traits in Mason, an energetic modernizer, who was straight speaking, knowledgeable and able, from the centre or centre right of the party. Mason may not have had the relatively privileged social, academic and professional background as Wilson but he was also a quick thinking Yorkshireman who could be trusted to do a good job in a variety of roles and responsibilities. He was hard working and always well prepared, confident with the media and capable in meetings. Both men of course were iconic pipe smokers.

The most significant international events associated with the 1964-70 Wilson government were the Unilateral Declaration of Independence of Rhodesia, France's veto of Britain's entry into the European Community, the Israeli-Arab war and America's continued involvement in Vietnam, the latter resulting in several major anti-war demonstrations. Serious civil unrest also began during the winter of 1968-69 in Northern Ireland, the British army taking over security and policing there the following August. In sport, the greatest achievement was the England football team winning the World Cup at Wembley on 30 July 1966.

Mason's first appointment, as a Minister of State at the Board of Trade, with special responsibility for shipping, came as something of a personal surprise as he had hoped for a more familiar position, that of Postmaster-General. However, it was a typically shrewd move by Wilson, the Barnsley MP given responsibility over a declining industry in tremendous need of reform. Mason quickly found out the huge, near impossible nature of the job, dealing with great but outdated shipyards, inept management and a myriad of restrictive practices from competing trade unions. A visit to Japan deepened his concerns and he was well aware that shipping operations in most European countries were miles ahead of Britain. Enthusiasm alone was no panacea for rapid change after the much quoted 'thirteen wasted years' of Tory government. Down to earth and practical, Mason instigated a review of shipbuilding and, whenever possible, tried to involve the predominantly Tory media in campaigns and innovations associated with safety at sea. However, even this approach nearly came a cropper when a publicity event involving a Grimsby trawler almost turned into a national tragedy in the rough waters of the North Sea. A reciprocal and routine visit to Russia, to meet their shipping minister, turned into a test of Anglo-Soviet relations when Mason was invited to meet the new Soviet prime minister, Aleksei Kosygin, in the Kremlin. A key part of the exchanges was not trade but the awkward question of Gerald Brooke, the young British lecturer who had been jailed for five years on a charge of smuggling religious and anti-Soviet literature.

Mason continued in the same post for a few months following the March 1966 general election when Labour achieved a 110-seat majority over the Conservatives. Industrial relations were at their lowest during the summer seamen's strike when Wilson saw their union leaders as politically motivated, attempting to destroy 'the welfare of the nation' and invoked a State of Emergency.

In January 1967 Mason was promoted to Minister of State for Defence Equipment. In his fifteen months at the MoD he got on well with Denis Healey, 'a formidably intelligent boss, a man who ran his department with the efficiency (though not necessarily the quietness) of a Rolls Royce engine'. Again, it was a new job at a difficult time. The government's economic measures to deal with inflation through a prices and incomes policy and a target of 4 per cent growth via the National Plan proved to be very optimistic. The inherited and record balance of payments deficit of £800m and pressure on the pound made reform in Wilson's 'white heat' of the 'scientific revolution' was more rhetoric than reality. Nevertheless, he was a high profile and loyal minister, making visits to a variety of military bases, even flying supersonic in a Lightening jet fighter. Perhaps the most memorable and commercially important overseas visit was to Tehran where he was given an audience with the Shah. It was towards the end of his work at the MoD that Mason was honoured when he was invited to become a member of the Privy Council. *Hansard* also reveals that he continued to raise items in respect of coal: pit closures in Scotland, redundancy, redeployment and new power stations.

After the cabinet reshuffle of April 1968 Wilson moved Mason from Defence to the role that he had expected four years earlier: Postmaster-General. Although in office barely three months, he ran the department with great energy and enthusiasm, even ordering a special stamp to be issued to commemorate the achievement of Celtic winning the European Cup. Philately remained a lifetime interest. One bit of controversy occurred in Parliament when, for safety reasons, he sanctioned the painting of Post Office engineers' vans yellow (from green), some members erroneously suspecting that post boxes and other features would have the same corporate treatment. Another was when his empathy towards post office workers' request for a pay increase ruffled feathers in the Treasury, and resulted in a summons to 11 Downing Street and a stern ticking off from Chancellor Roy Jenkins.

Mason's stay as Postmaster-General would have been longer but for the sudden resignation of the Minister of Power, Ray Gunter, in July 1968. Gunter, due to his personal problems, was proving to be an embarrassment to Wilson who saw Mason as the ideal replacement, running the industry in which the Barnsley man had worked as a youth and young adult. It also meant a place in the Cabinet. However, the ideal job was a nettle hard to grasp. Firstly, he would be inheriting a department that had not been run well. Secondly, the Cabinet had already agreed in principle to commission a new nuclear power station at Seaton Carew, near Hartlepool, close to the old Durham coalfield. The wave of condemnation from the miners and from people like Tony Benn and NCB Chairman Alfred Robens was predictable. Even the announcement was controversial, Mason instructed to involve the former Labour leader of Newcastle-upon-Tyne City Council, T Dan Smith, a powerful figure in the North-East who, although the son of miner, supported the project (but was subsequently convicted for bribery six years later). There was no compromise. Or was there? Mason told Wilson that he refused to grant a power station licence unless a coal-fired station was also built. By the end of his ministry Mason had secured a deal with the CEGB to licence four new stations, including the coal-fired Drax Two. Strategically placed near the new Selby coalfield in North Yorkshire, Drax began generation in 1974. Today (2008) it remains the largest single electricity generator in the UK. Lord Mason smiles when he reads about clean-coal technology forming a part of the present government's mixed bag of future energy choices.

The third major problem for Mason during his time at the Ministry of Power was the wave of pit closures which had already begun in earnest following the appointment of Alfred Robens as Chairman of the National Coal Board in 1961. Mason hated this situation and was frustrated at not having the power to stop the process. One strategy was an energy review conference he set up at Sunningdale after which the pit closure programme slowed. Egoistical Robens was warned about his future conduct by Mason following a mischievous television interview in which the NCB chairman breached his required neutral political status in favour of people such as newspaper magnate Cecil King and Lord Mountbatton and their apparent preference for a national government. Passages in Lord Robens' autobiography, *Ten Year Stint* (1972), show that he not only resented Mason's appointment but blamed him for harming the 'miners' morale' over Seaton Carew. Perhaps he was also thinking about the Mason reprimand too, not mentioned in his memoir.

A look at *Hansard* for the 1968-69 parliamentary session shows that Mason raised over 70 items in respect of the coal industry, including collieries, Drax B power station, manpower, redundancies, pit closures and the closure of an old Barnsley area pit: Wombwell Main. He also spoke about the Inquiry relating to the tragic events at Aberfan (21 October 1966) when 144 persons were killed, including 113 schoolchildren, when an unstable colliery spoil heap slid onto a local school. Earlier, in August 1967, several the NCB and several of its officers were censored for Aberfan and its Chairman, Alfred Robens, had offered his resignation to the then Minister of Power, Richard Marsh.

Mason's own stint ended almost as suddenly as his appointment fifteen months earlier when Power was absorbed into the new and huge Ministry of Technology under Tony Benn, in October 1969. Mason, however, remained in the cabinet, as President of the Board of Trade, a post that Wilson himself had occupied eighteen years earlier. It was a key job that involved a great deal of international contacts, seeking to improve trade. Unlike some ministers, he enjoyed the overseas travel, with Marjorie often in support. At home, keen to promote the regions, Mason steered colleagues in favour of building the new National Exhibition Centre in Birmingham, rather than in London as many businessmen and financiers preferred. An undoubted success, this was the start of the regional location and relocation of numerous national organisations from both the public and private sectors.

Hansard shows that Mason's duties were far ranging and frequent, from agriculture and aviation to trawling and Zambia, over 150 items listed in one, shortened (Oct-May) parliamentary session (1969/70).

Mason recalls cabinet meetings at this time being far from harmonious when discussing Barbara Castle's controversial White Paper *In Place of Strife*, which would have placed legal restrictions on unofficial strikes and inter-union disputes but also alienated their support of the Labour Party. The Bill, to Mason's relief, was dropped in June 1969 in return for the TUC's cautious undertaking to intervene in industrial disputes.

Boxing Day 1969 was a very happy day for the Masons when their oldest daughter, Susan, married Allen Duke in St Mary's Church, Barnsley.

In the Spring of 1970 there was optimism about Labour's popularity and confidence in Wilson winning a third term. However, poor trade figures, openly published without spin just before the election, were not helpful for the campaign, though Labour was already behind in the polls. Nevertheless the election defeat on 18 June came as a great shock for the Party as well as for Minister Mason who found himself - at least initially - 'disheartened and upset', back in Opposition after a remarkable taste of high office.

Life in Pictures

(1) Minister of State (Shipping & Tourism), 1964-67

Harold Wilson, seen here at a 1960s Yorkshire Miners' Gala, was elected as Labour's new and youngest ever Leader on 14 February 1963, defeating George Brown in the final vote. Described by his biographer Ben Pimlott as 'the most effective Leader of the Opposition of the twentieth century', Mason also found him 'clever and confident, with more than enough guile to hold the extremists in check...a truly formidable Leader of the Opposition'. (BEC)

On home ground, Mason had a convincing win in his safe Barnsley constituency, on a rainy 16 October 1964, obtaining 37,250 votes, a few thousand less than in 1959 but an almost 50% Labour majority over the Tory and Liberals. He is pictured here with Joan Hall (Conservative) and John Dossett (Liberal). Nationally, Labour scraped in with the narrowest of margins, a Commons majority of just five seats, but ending three successive election defeats and thirteen years of opposition. (Barnsley Chronicle)

ALL SET FOR THE BATTLE AHEAD

Mason's appointment was, for him, 'unknown territory', at the Board of Trade, under the much respected Douglas Jay, with responsibility for shipping and tourism (with aviation added later). It was a canny move by Wilson who was keen to modernise traditional industries, perhaps nowhere more disadvantaged than in the great yards of Clydeside, Tyneside and Belfast. One of Mason's first tasks, in January 1965, was a fact-finding visit to Tokyo. The smiling publicity shot is with a geisha girl but he was even more worried about the parlous state of British shipbuilding. 'There was not,' said Mason, 'a single job in shipbuilding which they couldn't do faster, more efficiently and cheaper'. He soon also found that the Danes and Russians were also way ahead. (MA)

A committee set up by Mason, highlighted the great need for a massive overhaul of the shipping industry. One of its members, astutely appointed so as to be aware of matters relating to redundancies, was Lancashire NUM Area Secretary Joe Gormley, recently elected on the NEC of the Party who, in 1971, became President of the miners' union. This cartoon by Waite, published in the *Sun* newspaper, 8 March 1966, illustrates the state of the shipbuilding industry - even poor old Noah had to wait! (MCA/Waite/The Sun)

Safety at sea was an important issue addressed - and experienced - by Mason during his junior minister's time at the Board of Trade. On one notable occasion he embarked on the Grimsby trawler *Ross Tern*, along with parliamentary colleague George Deer plus an assortment of journalists and broadcasters, joining the small crew of fishermen. The overnight journey on the North Sea was a near disaster because of unexpected Force 8 gale. A Mayday was called but the vessel limped into harbour in the early hours of the morning, much to the relief of all concerned. Built in 1962, The *Ross Tern* was eventually lost in the Pentland Firth in 1972. (Courtesy of North East Lincolnshire County Library Service)

Making a point to PM Harold Wilson in the presence of naval officers at a Safety at Sea meeting. (MA)

Following his *Ross Tern* adventure, Mason instigated a nationwide 'Safety at Sea' competition in order to find a new lifejacket (cf the traditional cork 'neckbreaker' then in service) for use by trawlermen and merchant seamen. The winning design came from McLintocks, a specialist textile company from Barnsley. Lightweight and innovatory, the new jacket was unveiled by the Thames at Surbitan on 21 May 1965, Mason not only wearing the new equipment, but making a spectacular leap into the river, much to the delight of the assembled press and sea cadets. The specification included a facility whereby the wearer, conscious or not, was turned face-upwards and kept afloat prior to rescue. It also proved to be a much needed export success. (MA)

Mason made many appearances at the annual galas and demonstrations organised by the Yorkshire miners, especially when they were held in Barnsley. This example took place in 1965, the leading party shown walking towards Locke Park. Left to right at the front are: Sidney Schofield (NUM), Lord Collinson (TUC Chairman), Councillor A Butler (Mayor of Barnsley), Mrs Butler, Sam Bullough (NUM), George Brown MP (Secretary of State), Mrs Brown, Roy Mason MP and J T Leigh (NUM).

The enigmatic George Brown (centre) was Deputy Leader (and self-styled Deputy PM) of the Labour Party and as First Secretary of State for Economic Affairs headed a huge new department. I remember him speaking very well at the gala, and getting a good reception. In my photograph he is flanked by police and protection officers, a situation soon to become commonplace for Mason. (BEC)

Harold Wilson launched Labour's 1966 election manifesto on 1 March. The day after, Mason was already performing for the press on a 'Bootie', a home exerciser and folding cycle, when he opened the 6th Engineering Exhibition at the Queen's Hall, Leeds. It was the start of a very effective campaign. (MA)

On home ground: Mason, with wife Marjorie and daughters Susan and Jill in Barnsley, preparing election addresses prior to distribution in March 1966. (Roy Sabine)

'Vote for me and I'll get the coal in!' Another excellent 1966 election photograph by Roy Sabine showing Mason out canvassing with Councillor Arthur Butler. (Roy Sabine)

Marjorie and Roy Mason on their way to vote on 31 March 1966. (Roy Sabine)

BARNSLEY

Electorate 69,751. 1964: 69,658

*Mason, R. (Lab)	38,744
Hall, Miss J. V. (C)	12,456
Lab Majority	26,288

Total Vote 51,200, Turnout 73·4%—Lab 75·7%, C 24·3%—Maj 51·3%.
Swing +0·75%

No Change

1964: TOTAL VOTE 55,756 (80·0%)—Lab 37,250 (66·8%), C 9,417 (16·9%), L 9,089 (16·3%)—Lab Maj 27,833 (49·9%).

Mr. Roy Mason, Minister of State, Board of Trade from 1964, with special responsibility for shipping, tourism and travel. Returned at a by-election in March, 1953. Born April, 1924; educated at elementary schools and London School of Economics. Miner, 1938-53. Member of the Yorkshire Miners' Council, 1949-53; branch official National Union of Mineworkers, 1947-53.

Miss Joan Hall contested the constituency in 1964. Secretary. Born August, 1935; educated at Queen Margaret's School, Escrick Park, York, and Ashridge House of Citizenship, Berkhamsted.

At the 1966 election Mason once again had a substantial majority over the Conservative candidate Joan Hall who also stood in 1964. It was a great night for Labour, who won the general election with a majority of 96 seats. 'Now we have a clear mandate,' said Wilson. (The Times)

Soon back on ministerial duties, Mason is seen here just prior to flying to Moscow on what became his most demanding international assignment to date, 3 May 1966. It was a reciprocal visit to meet Viktor Bakaev, the Soviet Minister of Merchant Marine who had visited London in September 1965. The official schedule also included talks with Mr Kuzmin, Deputy Minister of Foreign Trade and a visit to see the port and shipyard at Leningrad. (The Times)

A most unexpected encounter took place early on Mason's Russian visit when he was summoned to a secret meeting in the Kremlin with Alexey Kosygin, the Soviet Premier, described by Mason as 'a grey, gaunt man of little presence'. Kosygin complained about the delay in supplying three ships, Mason's advisor Amos Sutcliffe explaining to him that many of the parts were in fact Russian and provided late. Wilson instructed Mason to raise the subject of Gerald Brooke, the young British lecturer jailed in April 1965 for five years on a charge of smuggling religious and anti-Soviet literature into the USSR. Brooke was eventually released in July 1969, after four years custody and under threat of a serious espionage charge, in exchange for Peter and Helen Koroger, two senior Soviet agents. (MA)

Returning to shipping matters, Mason is seen here at the wheel of the United Towing Company's new tug *Welshman*, at Tower Pier, London, its skipper, Norman Storey in the background, 17 November 1966. The vessel was commissioned for use in the North Sea oilfields. It was a situation in which he may have had mixed feelings since a little over a year earlier, 26 February 1965, speaking in Barnsley, he warned about the 'fantastic' expenditure of the North Sea oil and gas companies and a potential fuel price war which could have 'a quick and adverse effect upon the coal industry...'. (MA)

(2) Minister of State for Defence Equipment, 1967-68

Mason's role as a junior minister at the Board of Trade was extended to include civil aviation. It was while he was having dinner with officials from the state airline, British Overseas Airways Corporation (BOAC), discussing takeovers/orders for US aircraft (as typified in this cartoon) that he was summoned to No. 10 for a meeting with PM Wilson who, wearied by the seamen's strike, promoted Mason to the Ministry of Defence (Equipment), under Secretary of State Denis Healey. BOAC was merged with British European Airways in 1974 to form British Airways. (MCA/Horner)

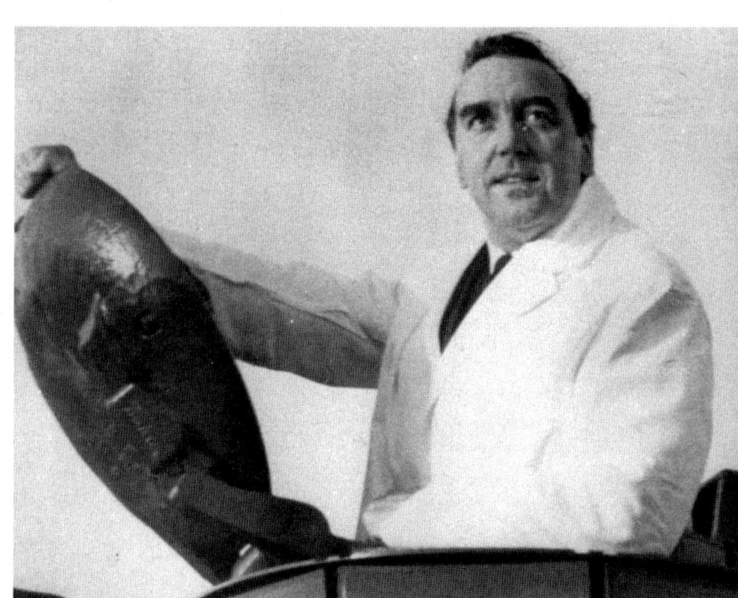

A few days after taking up his new post at the Ministry of Defence, on 13 January 1967, Mason visited the Royal Ordnance factory at Leeds where he was photographed in the cockpit of a Chieftain tank. (MA)

Plea to Europe to be more technically minded

Mr. Mason opens air traffic centre

In Paris, on 17 January 1967, opening a new air traffic experimental centre at Bretigny, which had a state of the art flight simulator (with possible links to the Concorde simulator at Toulouse), the result of European co-operation, and in line with Harold Wilson's vision of a 'European technological community'. (The Times)

Meeting Mohammed Reza Pahlavi, His Imperial Majesty, the Shah of Persia, in Tehran. The visit cemented a lucrative agreement to export 1,200 British tanks to Iran. The Shah was overthrown in the February revolution of 1979, when the Islamic Republic was declared. He died in exile, in Egypt, on 27 July 1980. (MA)

On 17 October 1967, following a rigorous health check, Mason became 'the Government's fastest and fittest Minister' when he flew in an English Electric Lightning supersonic fighter aircraft, from Coltisham, at 1,200 mph, therefore breaking the sound barrier. This photograph show the 43-year-old MP climbing into the cockpit. RAF Pilots likened flying the fighter as 'being saddled to a skyrocket'. This type was a T5, a 2-seat side-by-side training version.

The 1,000 Miles Per Hour Club

Whereas the 1,000 Miles Per Hour Club has been formed to honour those who have achieved this speed in an aircraft of conventional configuration

And whereas Mr. Roy Mason M.P. (hereinafter called "the New Member") has achieved this speed in the Lightning T5 aircraft

Now in pursuance of these presents and in consideration of the natural respect to which the New Member is entitled **this deed witnesseth** as follows:

1. **The** New Member is admitted, appointed and installed as a Life Member of the 1,000 Miles Per Hour Club together with all the rights and appurtenances thereto

2. **The** New Member is eligible and entitled to wear the official club tie at any time and in particular on those occasions when the claim of the Member is likely to be challenged **and further** the New Member is entitled to call upon other Members of the Club for aid and assistance in meeting and repelling the remarks defamatory or otherwise of Non-Members

In witness whereof the Common Seal of the Club has been hereunto affixed by Order of the Board of Management in the presence of

N. J. Galpin [illegible] Secretary

[illegible] Gp Capt President

17th OCTOBER 1967

Mason's jet-flying earned entry to an exclusive club, this membership certificate presented to him by Group Captain Hobson. Regular performers at air shows, Lightnings were also bought by the Kuwait and Royal Saudi air forces and continued in use by the RAF until retirement in 1988. (MA)

MRS. R. MASON

MRS. MASON LAUNCHES DESTROYER

Yesterday (Thursday) Mrs. Roy Mason, wife of the Barnsley M.P. and Minister of Defence (Equipment) became the first Barnsley housewife to have the privilege of launching a ship.

The "God speed to all who sail in her" ceremony took place at Fairfield's shipyard on the Clyde, when Mrs. Mason launched and named a Royal Navy guided missile destroyer, H.M.S. Antrim.

It was also a special occasion for her husband for while Mr. Mason has toured some 46 shipyards in Britain, Japan, Sweden and Russia, it was the first time he had ever seen a ship-launching ceremony — and, happily it was his wife who broke the traditional bottle of champagne against the new ship.

In his role at the Defence Ministry, Mr. Mason this week clocked up another "first" in his career—this time being a passenger on an R.A.F. Lightning which took him on a 1,200 m.p.h. trip over the North Sea.

On Tuesday he visited the R.A.F. Station at Coltisham, near Norwich, and went aboard a Lightning aircraft on an interception exercise. His 'plane carried him through the sound-barrier — "hardly noticeable when you are in the air"—and this earned him membership of an exclusive club for people who have gone through the barrier and have travelled at over 1,000 m.p.h.

Purpose of his visit was to experience at first-hand the handling of the aircraft and equipment—which he has to "sell" to foreign buyers—and a side-benefit was his need to undergo the "most rigorous medical" of his life before being allowed to fly; and the outcome was an A.1. report.

Just three days later, on 20 October 1967, Mason and his wife Marjorie were at Fairfield's shipyard on the Clyde, for the launch of the Royal Navy guided missile destroyer HMS *Antrim* (after County Antrim in Northern Ireland), Mrs Mason performing the naming ceremony. A Devonshire-class armoured cruiser, she was sold to the Chilean Navy in 1984 and renamed *Almirante Cochrane*. (Barnsley Chronicle)

'We are watching.' Mason also visited the RAF Fylingdales station on the North Yorkshire Moors which had been built by the Radio Corporation of America (RCA) a few years earlier, in 1962. Its purpose was to provide both countries with advanced knowledge of an impending ballistic missile attack, often referred to as the 'four-minute warning', during the Cold War. Three 40-metre-diameter 'golfballs' (radomes) made the site a highly distinctive landscape and 'tourist' feature. The domes were replaced by the present tetrahedron structure in 1989-92, housing sophisticated radar. (MA)

On what appears to be the same busy day Mason also visited and inspected a hovercraft. This army photograph, was part of a batch presented to the minister afterwards, from their Southern Command in Salisbury, Wiltshire. (MA)

At this time Mason, as a NUM-sponsored MP, received some criticism about his representation of local miners. The main source was the Woolley Colliery miners' branch and its young delegate, Arthur Scargill, the beginning of what Mason later described as 'an enduring enmity'. But, as can be seen from this report from the *Guardian* newspaper, Mason got the overwhelming support of the Yorkshire Area Council of the NUM, defeating the Woolley Colliery resolution by 93 votes to 8. A few days earlier, on 10 December 1967, the Barnsley Divisional Labour Party also gave him 'a unanimous vote of confidence...for the way he has been looking after mineworkers' interests'.
(The Guardian/Barnsley Chronicle)

Yorkshire miners support MP

The Yorkshire area council of the National Union of Mineworkers yesterday rejected by 93 votes to 8 a resolution from Woolley Colliery calling for withdrawal of financial support for Mr Roy Mason, Labour MP for Barnsley, and support for him at the next general election.

The Woolley miners were against what they said was Mr Mason's support of the Government's fuel policy.

Of the several overseas visits undertaken whilst Mason was in charge of Defence (Equipment) these two example shows him in talks in Rio de Janeiro, Brazil and visiting the Mitsubishi main engine works in Japan. (MA)

(3) Postmaster General (April 1968-June 1968)

Official photograph of the new Postmaster-General, at the GPO (General Post Office) headquarters in St Martins Le Grande, London. Mason replaced Edward 'Ted' Short. It proved to be a short stint, just three months, his successor being the ultimately notorious Wednesbury and later Walsall North MP John Stonehouse who, as 'Joseph Markham', faked his own death in 1974. The office of Postmaster-General was abolished in 1969, replaced with the post of Minister of Posts and Telecommunications.

Enjoying his new job: opening the Earth-Station Seminar at the Royal Lancaster Hotel, London, on 20 May 1968. Satellite communications was a subject that the minister had shown an active interest in over several years. This international event included exhibitors from fifty countries. The British satellite on show here is a scale model of Ariel 3 which had been in orbit for a year. (MA)

'How's business?' Mason embarked on a week's tour of UK scientific and industrial establishments following his official visit to the telecommunications exhibition but also found time, the day after (21 May), to call at a London sub-post office. His interest in the subject of stamp collecting (philately) continued over many years. (MA)

(4) Minister of Power, July 1968 - October 1969

An early morning call from Downing Street on 2 July 1968 summoned Mason to lunch at Chequers with the Prime Minister - meaning a long cab trip from Barnsley. The outcome was further promotion - following the sudden resignation of Ray Gunter - to his dream job of Minister of Power. Mason was now responsible for running the great industry where he once worked as a pit-lad for less than a pound a week, entering the Cabinet at the relatively young age of 44. This portrait image was taken after a visit to a Lancashire pit. (MA)

One of Mason's first VIP visitors to the Ministry of Power headquarters at Millbank was a young Prince Charles who was shown around the offices on the morning of 18 July 1968. An underground visit was also discussed. Thirty-two years later Lord Mason, still very much involved in the Prince's Trust, sent Charles a copy of the photograph, receiving a pleasing reply. (MA)

Nuclear power station decision dismays miners

A nuclear power station with a capacity of 1,250 megawatts is to be built at Seaton Carew, near Hartlepool, County Durham. The announcement yesterday by the Minister of Power, Mr Roy Mason, that the Government had consented to the Central Electricity Generating Board's application, brought to an end years of uncertainty about the project, and dealt a bitter blow to Lord Robens and Durham coal miners.

The National Coal Board has fought hard to win the contracts to fuel the station. It would have guaranteed the jobs of between 6,000 and 8,000 miners for the next 25 years.

For Hartlepool and Teesside, however, which need an extra 1,000 megawatts of electricity in the 1970s, the news is doubly welcome. The project will reduce unemployment—up to 2,400 men will be needed to build the station—and will provide an additional attraction to new industry.

The new minister considered instant resignation on hearing about the Cabinet's apparently unanimous decision to build a nuclear power station near to Seaton Carew on the Durham coalfield, heralding, he felt, 'the death-knell of coal'. Mason told Wilson that he would refuse to grant any new power station licences unless there was 'another coal-fired station back on stream'. However, the controversial decision to go ahead with nuclear power was announced in August 1968, receiving widespread press coverage. This typical headline appeared in the *Guardian*.

Construction work began at the Seaton Carew (near Hartlepool) site in the summer of 1969 and generation began in 1983. Operated by British Energy, it is scheduled for decommissioning by 2014. (Maureen Anderson)

Mason was an understandably uneasy Minister of Power in context of a massive programme of pit closures, well under way under the authority of the National Coal Board chaired by the former Labour minister Lord Robens (appointed in 1961), who oversaw the closure of 400 pits in his ten-year term of office, along with the loss of one in every two miners' jobs. About 30 closures took place during Mason's ministry. Robens is seen here in 1970 at one of his new showpiece Yorkshire mines, Riddings Drift. The miner with Robens is Des Spencer who had previously worked at Wombwell Main, an old Barnsley area pit, which the NCB closed in May 1969. (BEC)

The official Wilson Cabinet photograph, October 1968. Left to right, standing; Judith Hart, George Thomas, Cledwyn Hughes, Richard Marsh, Edward Short, William Ross, George Thompson, Tony Benn, Anthony Greenwood, Lord Shackleton, Roy Mason, John Diamond and Sir Burke Trend. Left to right, seated: Peter Shore, Denis Healey, Barbara Castle, Lord Gardiner, Michael Stewart, Harold Wilson, Roy Jenkins, Richard Crossman, James Callaghan, Fred Peart and Anthony Crossland. (MA)

Pit visits were a regular occurrence while Mason was Minister of Power. This early example to an unidentified colliery may even pre-date his new post. Here, he has been well-kitted for the occasion, perhaps appropriately so in view of the emphasis on safety displayed in the background. His clean-looking appearance contrasts with the two pitmen, so the underground journey may not have started. (MA)

Here, Mason is visiting his old pit, Wharncliffe Woodmoor 4 & 5, at Carlton, near Barnsley.

In this close-up picture he is wearing a miners' neck scarf, his appearance suggesting that he has been underground. Wharncliffe Woodmoor 4 & 5 Colliery closed in June 1970, towards the end of Robens' ten-year stint at the National Coal Board. (MA)

On this occasion Mason is seen after visiting a Lancashire pit (NCB North-Western Region) in the presence of NUM Area General Secretary (and national executive) Joe Gormley (seated, 2nd left). Mason's suit looks worse for wear after the underground excursion. Three years later, Gormley was elected President of the NUM. (BEC)

Mason at the coal face of a Lancashire pit. Note the white 'VIP' overalls on this occasion. (BEC)

This unusual triple-image was referred to as 'The Minister in a Powerful Act' in a press release. It shows the Minister of Power testing safety equipment, namely (left to right) a 'self-rescuer' (breathing apparatus), earphones (listening) and a magnification instrument. It took place on a visit to the Safety in Mines Research Establishment at Sheffield, on 2 January 1969. (MA)

The leading party approaching Kingstone during the march to Locke Park at the Yorkshire Miners' Gala and Demonstration, Barnsley, Saturday 21 June 1969. The whole of Racecommon Road, one of the longest streets in town, is full of people and banners. The leaders include (left to right) Lawrence Daly (NUM), Bill Paynter (NUM), Roy Mason MP (centre), the Mayor and Mayoress (Councillor & Mrs Theodore Hinchliffe) and Sydney Schofield (Yorkshire NUM). (BEC)

Typically smart, Mason poses for the NCB photographer prior to speaking at the 1969 Yorkshire Miners' Gala. (BEC)

Mason, seen here in animated form was guest speaker at the 1969 Yorkshire Miners' Gala (along with NUM Secretary Lawrence Daly), an event which attracted a large crowd to Barnsley's Locke Park. (BEC)

A variety of personal objects relating to the 1968/69 period when Roy Mason was Minister of Power can be seen at Cawthorne Village Museum, near Barnsley: Black ministerial brief case engraved 'Minister of Power' and address of his Millbank offices. Miner's safety lamp, presented to Roy Mason on the occasion of his visit to Wentworth Silkstone Colliery, 6 June 1969. (BEC) Lord Mason holding 'red box No 9', inscribed 'Minister of Power'. (BEC) Lord Mason wearing his 'Minister of Power' pit helmet and well-used pit boots. (BEC)

1968-69 Cmnd. 3888 **In Place of Strife: A Policy for Industrial Relations (Industrial Relations)**

265

IN PLACE OF STRIFE

A POLICY FOR INDUSTRIAL RELATIONS

Presented to Parliament by the First Secretary of State and
Secretary of State for Employment and Productivity
by Command of Her Majesty
January 1969

LONDON
HER MAJESTY'S STATIONERY OFFICE
3s. 6d. net

Cmnd. 3888

Barbara Castle's controversial White Paper *In Place of Strife* which proposed a series of legal restrictions on the right of workers to strike was introduced to the Cabinet in early 1969. By June, Mason had already decided that it would 'suicidal' for the reforms to go ahead, alienating the trade unions, part of a groundswell of opposition, led by his mentor James Callaghan, which led to the abandonment of the Castle proposals. Mason later described this period as 'wearisome months of rows, rumours, negotiations, disagreements in Cabinet and mutterings against the Prime Minister'. 'She [Castle] should have called it [her paper]', he said, 'In Place of Common Sense. It was a disaster...and did more to undermine morale within the government and the party than any other event in Harold Wilson's first six years. (MA)

erhaps the personal highlight f the year 1969 was when Roy and Marjorie Mason hosted a eception at Downing Steet for the American astronauts Neil Armstrong, Edwin 'Buzz' Aldrin and Michael Collins, resh from the Apollo 11 moon anding of 20/21 July, and part their 'Great Leap' world tour. Mason had had a long-time nterest in space travel and as a ung backbencher had met the irst man and woman in space, Yuri Gagarin and Valentina Tereshkova. (MA)

(5) President of the Board of Trade, October 1969 - June 1970

Mason remained in the Cabinet as President of the Board of Trade. He succeded Anthony Crosland following the absorption of the Ministry of Power into the new and vast Ministry of Technology, under Tony Benn, on 6 October 1969. Wilson moved Crosland to Local Government and Regional Planning. (MA)

The nature of the new job entailed a great deal of overseas travel, something that Mason always enjoyed, meeting leading politicians and heads of state. Here he can be seen with His Majesty King Hussein of Jordan. (MA)

Mason in Malta, with Marjorie, welcomed by the leader and founder of its Labour Party, Dom Mintoff. Malta had been granted independence from Britain on 21 September 1964 though ties with Britain remained close, even after a republic was declared in 1974.

In Valetta, by the plaque commemorating the award of the George Cross to the 'Island Fortress' in 1942. (MA)

Roy and Marjorie Mason (extreme right) waiting behind the Queen and Queen Mother to be greeted by the Marshal of the Royal Air Force, Sir Andrew Humphrey, at a Guildhall dinner in 1969. (MA)

Working on state papers in the garden of his Barnsley home during the election campaign, 2 June 1970. (Roy Sabine)

'Try a tomato Mrs...and don't forget to vote for me...' Electioneering and canvassing for votes on Barnsley Market at the eve of the 1970 General Election, 18 June. (Roy Sabine)

Part Five

No More Red Boxes
Opposition, 1970-74

'There is something liberating about losing office, once the initial disappointment has worn off.'

Weighing the catch after a day's sea fishing at Bridlington, as a guest of Barnsley Sea Angling Club. Opposition provided Mason with a little more time to participate in one of his great outdoor passions. He also discovered the joys of fly fishing which was to become a lifetime interest. (MA)

Life and Times

1970 [6.] Wharncliffe Woodmoor 4 & 5 Colliery, Mason's former pit, closes.
Wilson appoints Mason as Principal Opposition Spokesman on Board of Trade Affairs.
Mason appoints new East Hull MP John Prescott as front-bench Labour Spokesman on Shipping.
Member of Council of Europe, 1970-71.
Chairman of Yorkshire Group of Labour MPs, 1970-74.
Visits China, leading an all-party delegation.
[5.10] Campaigns for a National Transport Museum for York.

1971 [21.2] Massive trade union opposition in London to government's Industrial Relations Bill.
[25.2] Important Commons speech about unemployment in Barnsley 'and the coal zone'.
[4.10] Labour Party Conference opposes entry into European Economic Community (EEC) 'on existing terms'.
[28.10] Mason one of 69 Labour 'pro-market rebels' who voted with the Tories in support of EEC membership.

1972 [9.1] National strike of mineworkers starts and includes the deployment of 'flying pickets', notably at the Saltley Marsh Coal Depot in the West Midlands.
[20.1] Unemployment in UK passes one million mark.
[22.1] Britain joins European Economic Community (EEC).
[30.1] 'Bloody Sunday' in Londonderry, 14 civilians killed by British Parachute Regiment during a civil rights march.
[10.2] Battle of Saltley Gate, Birmingham.
[9/11.2.] State of Emergency declared by Conservative government and a three-day week imposed to save energy.
[11.2] Wilberforce Inquiry into mineworkers' pay.
[22.2] IRA attack at Aldershot kills 5 women cleaners, a gardener and a Catholic priest; Mason and 50 Labour MPs tables motion abhorring the conduct of those responsible.
[25.2] Miners' strike officially called off and mineworkers now head the industrial wages table.
[4.3] Hovercraft capsizes in Solent killing five people.
[10.12] Mason is keynote speaker, stressing the importance of regional development at a conference in Leeds

1973 [1] Mason meets Emperor Haile Selassie, during an 8-day visit to Ethiopia.
[21.3] Lofthouse pit disaster, near Wakefield, 6 killed.
[8.4] Mason campaigns to keep Barnsley's traditional brewery from closure.
[4.5] Mason flies supersonic in prototype of Concorde.
[1.9] Mason proposes a national disaster corps to co-ordinate rescue efforts

		at major aircraft, rail and motor accidents.
	[6.10]	War in the Middle East and oil crisis.
	[15.12]	Mason is new chairman of miners' group of MPs.
	[31.12]	Heath Government imposes 3-day week.
1974	[7.2]	'Who governs Britain?' Heath calls General Election
	[8.2]	Willie Whitelaw, Secretary for Employment appeals to Mason as chairman of miners' group of MPs for miners to accept 'the very reasonable offer'.
	[9.2.]	Miners strike again due to the erosion of their last pay award.
	[28.2]	General Election: Labour wins 301 seats, 4 more than the Conservatives, but both parties unable to form a majority government. Mason retains his Barnsley seat for a sixth time, polling 40,595 votes (24,626 majority).
	[1.3]	Heath unsuccessfully appeals to Liberals for support.
	[6.3]	Harold Wilson forms minority Labour government, his second administration.

Overview

In his mid-forties and already with a wealth of political experience and responsibility, Mason was understandably despondent at his loss of office. Had Labour won in 1970 it is likely that he would have been appointed to another senior cabinet post. His achievements had been considerable. But there were compensations. Opposition provided a little more time with Marjorie and his family; and more opportunity for constituency work, charity involvement and leisure interests, particularly fishing, an activity which gave him immense enjoyment, out in the countryside with old and new friends. Along with his pipe, fishing was a pleasure that helped him relax during stressful times, no more so than when he was back in office, with massive responsibilities.

However, Opposition was by no means a politically inactive period. There was lots of valuable constituency work to do, as well as charity involvement. It was at this time that Mason started arranging free monthly film shows in Barnsley for pensioners and the disabled, a much appreciated facility that continued until a few years ago; and a series of specially adapted powered wheelchairs, designed by Lord Snowden, were funded from voluntary contributions through Mason's enthusiastic campaign.

As chairman of the Yorkshire group of Labour MPs at this time Mason was keen to advocate the establishment of a new, what was sometimes described in the media as a national 'transport museum' based in York rather than London. The campaign proved to be successful, the National Railway Museum (NRM) opening at York in 1975, not long after Labour's return to power. The NRM became the first national museum outside of London. It has won many awards and now attracts around 850,000 visitors a year.

Mason had always been a pro-European but the decision of the Labour Party Conference, in October 1971, to oppose entry on present terms, left him labelled 'a rebel' when, along with 69 colleagues he voted with the Tories to join the Common

Market. The most senior Labour MP to defy the three-line whip was Roy Jenkins, no doubt annoyed by Wilson's earlier promise of a free vote according to conscience. Earlier, although under heavy fire from the National Union of Mineworkers, Mason published the pamphlet *Coal and the Common Market* (8 September 1971) in which he accused his union of opposing entry 'without even assessing the terms' and stating that the Market was, in the face of increasingly competitive trade combined with Tory [pit closure] policy 'the salvation of the British coal industry'.

Working as Labour's spokesperson for Board of Trade, Mason remained on the front bench, keen as ever to express his views during Commons debates, tabling motions and questions on local, regional and national issues. One of his first junior appointments was a grateful John Prescott, 32-year-old former seaman who had been just been elected for Hull East. Prescott was to become Deputy Prime Minister and a leading figure in successive Blair governments. Mason's Opposition team also included two other notable new MPs: Albert Booth (Barrow-in-Furness) who went on to become Secretary of State for Employment in the forthcoming Callaghan cabinet and Stanley Clifton Davis (Hackney Central), a future European Commissioner.

Mason had always enjoyed travel and several overseas visits took place, most notably to China, when he led a delegation, one of the first in the wake of Chairman Mao's Cultural Revolution. He was also one of the last politicians to meet King and Emperor Haile Selassie in Ethiopia, at a time when parts of his kingdom were experiencing terrible famine, retrospectively regarded as the world's first 'televised catastrophe'.

Burgeoning unemployment, particularly in old industrial and coal mining areas also gave Mason plenty of opportunity to contribute at local meetings and regional conferences; and, as we have seen, was never afraid to speak his mind during disputes despite NUM sponsorship. Following a decision of the North Yorkshire miners' panel vote for a resumption of work during the November 1970 unofficial pay dispute Mason urged the outstanding strikers to return 'for economic reasons'. Shortly afterwards, in January 1971, following a meeting in Barnsley with redundant mineworkers, he spoke about a 'vast army of forgotten men' who were worried about taking jobs under industrial training schemes due to the loss of benefits provided under the Coal Industry Act. Mason, albeit with other Labour MPs, even joined a secondary picket shortly after the start of the 1972 miners' strike. The landmark Battle of Saltley Gate in the West Midlands was forecast when he pleaded for the depot gates to be closed to all but essential traffic 'or clashes with the police will be inevitable'. Mason had expressed hope that the pickets would 'act responsibly'. The police's decision to shut the coke depot was generally hailed as a landmark victory for the striking miners, in particular for the strategy of its upcoming leader Arthur Scargill. Animosity between the two continued to grow. In parliament, Mason continued to highlight the dangerous conditions in which miners worked (92 killed and 600 seriously injured in 1971) and the hundreds dying every year from respiratory diseases, referring to Tory ministers' policies in relation to coal miners as 'short-sighted, stupid, doctrinaire and provocative'.

The Conservative government's attitude to nationalised organisations had also come under criticism from Mason when the Thomas Cook travel firm (then nationalised) was scheduled to be sold off to private industry in November 1971. Travel companies were, said Mason, 'queuing up to make their bids', envisaging 'rich pickings'. Better, he thought, for Cook's to be transferred to join the BOAC-BEA travel service, in public ownership.

The growing civil unrest in Northern Ireland ('Bloody Sunday' in Londonderry had taken place only a few days before the start of the 1972 miners' strike) and the IRA bombing of the Parachute Brigade headquarters at Aldershot in which five cleaning women, a gardener and a Catholic priest were killed resulted in condemnation from Mason in speeches in parliament. On 22 February Mason was one of the leading Labour MPs who tabled a motion 'abhorring the conduct of those who caused the deaths and injuries in Aldershot'.

Always interested in modern modes of transport, Mason spoke in the Commons following an accident in the Solent when a hovercraft capsized, killing five people (4 March 1972). He emphasised the 'remarkable safety record' of the vessels, saying that the accident may have been 'an unusual combination of freak wind and wave conditions'.

In 1973, Mason wrote to the Prime Minister suggesting the formation of a 'national disaster corps' to co-ordinate rescue efforts at major aircraft, rail and motor accidents. He proposed that civil and military organisations would function best if they were unified 'for contingency planning'.

The announcement by Tadcaster-based John Smith's (part of the Imperial Tobacco group) to phase out the brewing of famous ales such as Barnsley Bitter and Old Tom in his home town of Barnsley resulted in a flurry of local and parliamentary activity by Mason during the early and mid-1970s. Although he was unable to halt the process, his vigourous campaigning, which attracted a lot of media interest, was also against the increasingly monopolistic powers of the 'big brewers' nationwide. In this he was heartily supported by the Campaign for the Real Ale (CAMRA) who claimed that the North of England would become a 'beer drinkers wilderness' unless urgent action was taken to prevent the takeover and closure of local breweries. Over 12,000 people signed petitions to keep the brewery open but the last brew of 'Oakwell Ales - Pure as a Spring' - took place in 1976.

Berating the lack of former trade union men in the Cabinet, Tony Benn referred to Mason as 'an amiable guy but as he gets older and absorbed into the parliamentary system, his early left-wing ideas are beginning to be eroded' in a diary entry of 9 October 1973 (Benn, 2, 68).

During the impending miners' strike of 1974 Mason referred to the 'government intransigence' and 'confrontation' attitude of Heath and the Tories which 'openly challenged' the miners 'and played into the hands of people like Mick McGahey and Arthur Scargill...' Mason, as chairman of the miners' group of Labour MPs, along with the group secretary, Elfed Davies, was called into a secret meeting with the Secretary of State for Employment, Willie Whitelaw. Whitelaw refused to accept that the miners were a 'special case' or to recognise that they had to spend time waiting to go underground and to bathe after shifts. The enigmatic Conservative, Enoch Powell, in a speech in Derby, called on Heath to abandon his own personal pride and admit that Stage Three (of the Prices and Incomes policy) was a mistake, otherwise the country would 'face a real disaster'. The fall of the Heath government at the 'who governs Britain' election a few weeks later confirmed Mason's and Powell's analysis. It was the also the eve of the most challenging period of Roy Mason's political and personal life.

BARNSLEY

Electorate 75,743. 1966: 69,751

Mason, R. (Lab)	34,956
odber, R. (C)	10,811
ossett, J. H. (L)	8,186
Lab majority	24,145

otal Vote 53,953, Turnout 71%—Lab 64·8%, C 20·0%, L 15·2%—Lab maj 44·8%. Swing +3·1%

o Change

966: Total Vote 51,200 (73·4%)—Lab 38,744 (75·7%), C 12,456 (24·3%)—Lab maj 26,288 (51·3%).

Mr. Roy Mason was resident of the Board f Trade from 1969-70. linister of Power, 968-69; Postmaster ieneral, April-June, 968; Minister of Denee (Equipment), 967-68; Minister of tate, Board of Trade 964-67. Returned at a y-election in March, 953. B April, 1924; ed t elementary schools and London School of conomics. Miner, 1938-53. Member, Yorkiire Miners' Council, 1949-53; branch fficial, NUM 1947-53.

Mr. Robert Godber, teacher. B July, 1942; d Ecclesfield Grammar School and Manhester University. Chairman, Yorkshire 'oung Conservatives.

Mr. John H. Dossett, contested the seat, 964. Engineering company manager. B December, 1931; ed Barnsley Grammar chool.

Abstract of the 1970 General Election result for the Barnsley constituency, from *The Times Guide to the House of Commons 1970*. (The Times)

ohn Prescott, former ship's steward and National Union of Seamen (NUS) official, became MP for Hull East (sponsored by his union) after the 1970 general election and was appointed by Mason as Opposition shipping spokesperson, 'Because he was good. He came in with all his experience in ipping [and] he knew his subject.' Prescott's first experience at the Dispatch Box, deputising for Mason, took place on 6 May 1971 when he spoke mpetently about safety at sea. Prescott became a ading figure in the Blair government, appointed Deputy Prime Minister in 1997 (to 2007). (BEC)

Mason's constituency work at this time included contacts and help with a variety of charities and good causes, an aspect of his life that Marjorie had great interest. Here Roy and Marjorie can be seen in the foyer of the Ritz Cinema in Barnsley presenting a 'chairmobile' to multiple sclerosis sufferer Andrew Salter (front, 2nd left, next to his mother, Barbara) who had two brothers (Ralph and Duncan, sat next to Andrew) also affected by the disease. An able-bodied brother, Clive, can be seen holding Andrew's chair. The event was later described by Mason as 'the happiest [moment] of my political life'. Eventually a total of thirteen of the innovatory machines, designed by Lord Snowden, were provided for local disabled people. (MA)

A closer view of Andrew Salter and his new 'chairmobile', Roy Mason at the controls. (MA)

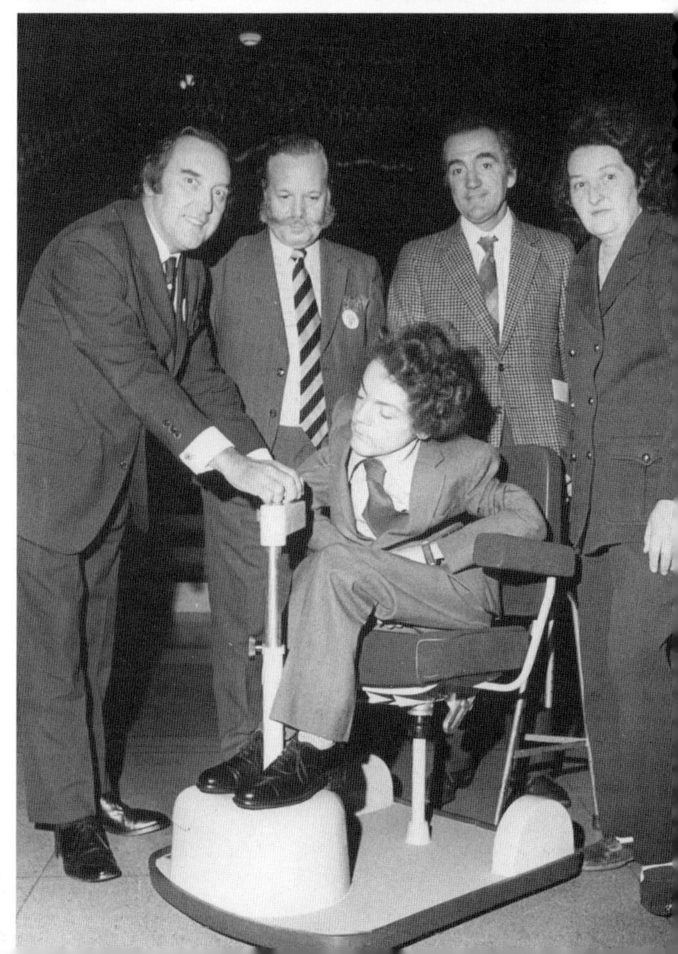

What about a new power station to llow Drax 2? We have the water, the el and the manpower. There would be 500 jobs during construction and 750 ereafter. If necessary, a new power ation could be tied to the new super-ine and if there were a deliberate in-stment decision by the Government, the ational Coal Board and the C.E.G.B. do this, it could rejuvenate the coal ne and quickly make an impact on the rious level of unemployment.

In the Yorkshire and Humberside egional Strategy Report, prepared by e Yorkshire and Humberside Economic lanning Council, reference is made to e serious situation in the coalfield—oncaster, Hemsworth, South Kirby, earne Valley and the Five Towns. My on. Friends the Members for Dearne alley (Mr. Edwin Wainwright) and Pon-fract (Mr. Harper) are present tonight ecause of the serious question of unem-loyment in their areas.

There is a special reference to Barnsley paragraph 135 :

"A reduction in labour demand is expected s a result of a continuing decline of employment in coalmining and a substantial shortage of male jobs is likely. In our report 'Employment Prospects in the Yorkshire Coalmining Areas', we recognised that the situation in Barnsley was particularly urgent."

It is still urgent and it is getting worse.

There is too much migration of young adults, professional workers and non-manual workers. Prospects for school-leavers are depressing. The elderly unemployed coal miner is destined to tread the streets hopelessly searching for work until ultimately he loses his pride and his soul. The after-effects of being dependent on a mono-economy in the area for so long is now hurting. New industries are badly needed and only by Government decree are these awful trends to be arrested.

Giving us full development status would help, and the extra financial incentives might start an inflow of industry. We have the sites and the manpower. Now it has become so desperate that we do not want just sympathy and hope from the Minister tonight—we want direct action.

Final page of Roy Mason's published speech in the Commons relating to unemployment in Barnsley and the coal zone of Yorkshire, 25 February 1971. The unemployment rate in Barnsley had reached 5.6% (cf 3.1% nationally) largely due to pit closures. (MA)

Fate of rebels in hands of constituencies

By MALCOLM STUART

After the vote—the possibi-ty of marching orders. Rebels f both parties are aware that he Common Market vote has ome at a particularly vulner-ble time for their continued ature as MPs.

Mason was one of 69 rebel Labour MPs (including Roy Jenkins) who voted in favour of Britain's membership of the Common Market (rather than voting against the terms of entry) on 28 October 1971. It was the first time that he had defied the Labour whip. Earlier, on 8 September, he had the courage to speak out against the NUM's rejection of EEC membership, arguing in a pamphlet that the coal industry would actually benefit. This headline, dated 30 October 1971, discussed the uncertainties and criticism that some of the rebels faced back in their constituencies. (The Guardian)

Following a pithead ballot, the miners went on an all-out official strike for better pay on 9 January 1972. All 289 pits closed and the NUM authorised secondary picketing, initially at coal-fired power stations, and then at all power stations, steelworks, ports and other strategic sites. Here Mason can be seen sharing a battered brazier outside Battersea Power Station with picketing miners Hedley Crewe (centre) and Grant Pew from Betteshanger Colliery (Kent), on 2 February. Parliamentary business meant that it was a fairly short 'publicity picket' for Mason and fourteen other NUM-sponsored MPs who also attended, though Bolsover MP Dennis Skinner's solidarity extended to a couple of hours. (MA)

Police struggling to keep control of thousands of miners, engineering and transport workers in a mass picket outside Saltley coke depot in the West Midlands at the start of the fifth week of the miners' strike and just two days after Prime Minister Edward Heath's declaration of a state of emergency. For one young former Woolley miner named Arthur Scargill, Saltley was a 'blacklegging depot' which had to shut. Having coordinated mobile or 'flying' pickets via the Barnsley Strike Committee, Scargill saw the closure as a great victory for the miners he represented and 'the greatest day of my life'. (BEC)

The inquiry into miners' pay, set up on 11 February and chaired by Lord Wilberforce, sat for just two days, starting on 15 February when this demonstration marched through London. Wilberforce conceding just about all the miners' grievances. A substantial pay package equivalent to 21 per cent was recommended and, following a ballot, the strike was called off on 28 February. Joe Gormley and the National Union of Mineworkers had won their case for 'A Living Wage' against Derek Ezra and the National Coal Board, a resolute defeat for the 'strong and honest government' promised by Edward Heath. (BEC)

Roy and Marjorie in Tiananmen Square with the ever present portrait of Mao Zedong in the background. Mason led a small delegation to China, one of the first international visits in the aftermath of the Cultural Revolution and prior to US President Nixon's well publicised trip of 1972. (MA)

His Imperial Majesty Haile Selassie (whose titles also included Conquering Lion of the Tribe of Judah, King of Kings of Ethiopia and Elect of God) welcomes Marjorie and Roy Mason during their 8-day visit to Ethiopia, 26 January 1973. They had flown to Addis Ababa on an inaugural direct flight from London. Once exiled in the UK (1936-41), Haile Selassie was 80 years old when he received the Masons, and the longest serving head of state in the world. It was a difficult time, however. Famine ravaged through the Wollo area, affecting the emperor's popularity and authority, starving families featured in a pioneering Jonathan Dimbleby television documentary. Selassie died on 28 August 1975 but continued to be worshipped as the living God incarnate among followers of the Rastafari movement. (Barnsley Chronicle)

Mason's long interest in aviation was further rewarded in 1973 when he was invited by the British Aircraft Corporation to be a VIP passenger on a Concorde demonstration flight from RAF Fairford. Here Mason can be seen inspecting some of the onboard equipment. A certificate, signed by the extrovert chief pilot Brian Tubshaw, was presented afterwards. Concorde's maiden flight had taken place in 1969, operational service commencing in 1976 (to 2003). (MA)

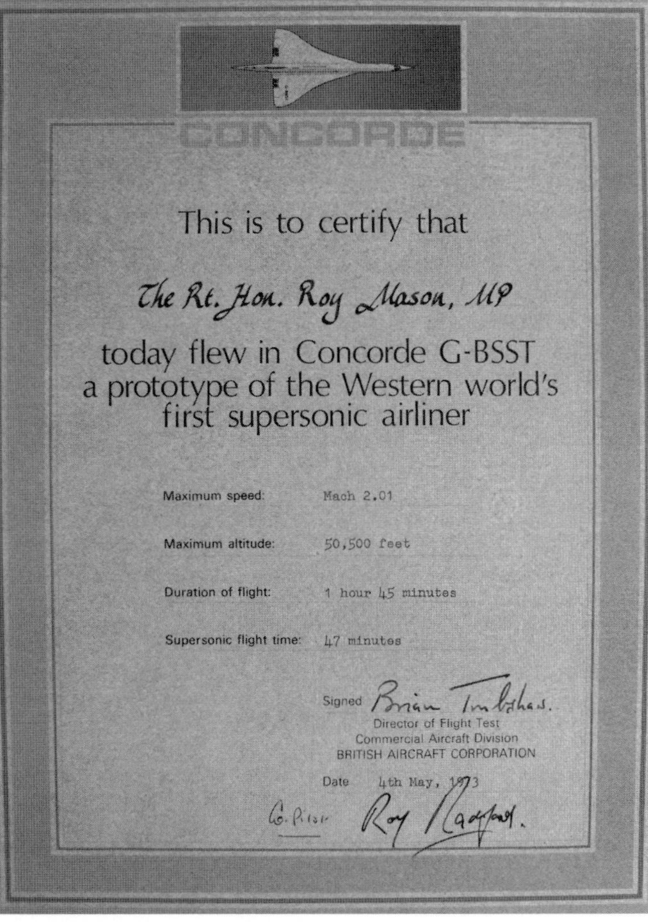

CONCORDE

This is to certify that

The Rt. Hon. Roy Mason, MP

today flew in Concorde G-BSST
a prototype of the Western world's
first supersonic airliner

Maximum speed: Mach 2.01

Maximum altitude: 50,500 feet

Duration of flight: 1 hour 45 minutes

Supersonic flight time: 47 minutes

Signed *Brian Tubshaw.*
Director of Flight Test
Commercial Aircraft Division
BRITISH AIRCRAFT CORPORATION

Date 4th May, 1973

The closure of Barnsley's Oakwell brewery by John Smith's of Tadcaster resulted in a bitter reaction from the Barnsley MP. A local poet summed up the mood in May 1973:

Now Barnsley Brewer's closing down.

Why not close the bloody town.

More than 12,000 people including the mayor had signed a petition against closure. Mason requested a meeting with Sir John Partridge, chairman of the Smith's parent company, the giant Imperial Tobacco group, to try and get him to overrule the decision. In the Commons Mason used the demise of Barnsley Brewery as an example of what was happening elsewhere in the country, getting 160 of his colleagues' signatures towards a motion for a parliamentary debate. A new clause against the monopoly powers of brewers in the Fair Trading Bill was drafted. Mason is seen here wearing a new tie that he had designed for the campaign, showing a symbolic sword of Damocles hanging over a pint of bitter. Note the sideburns which, combined with his pipe, were ideal fodder for cartoonists of the day. (MA)

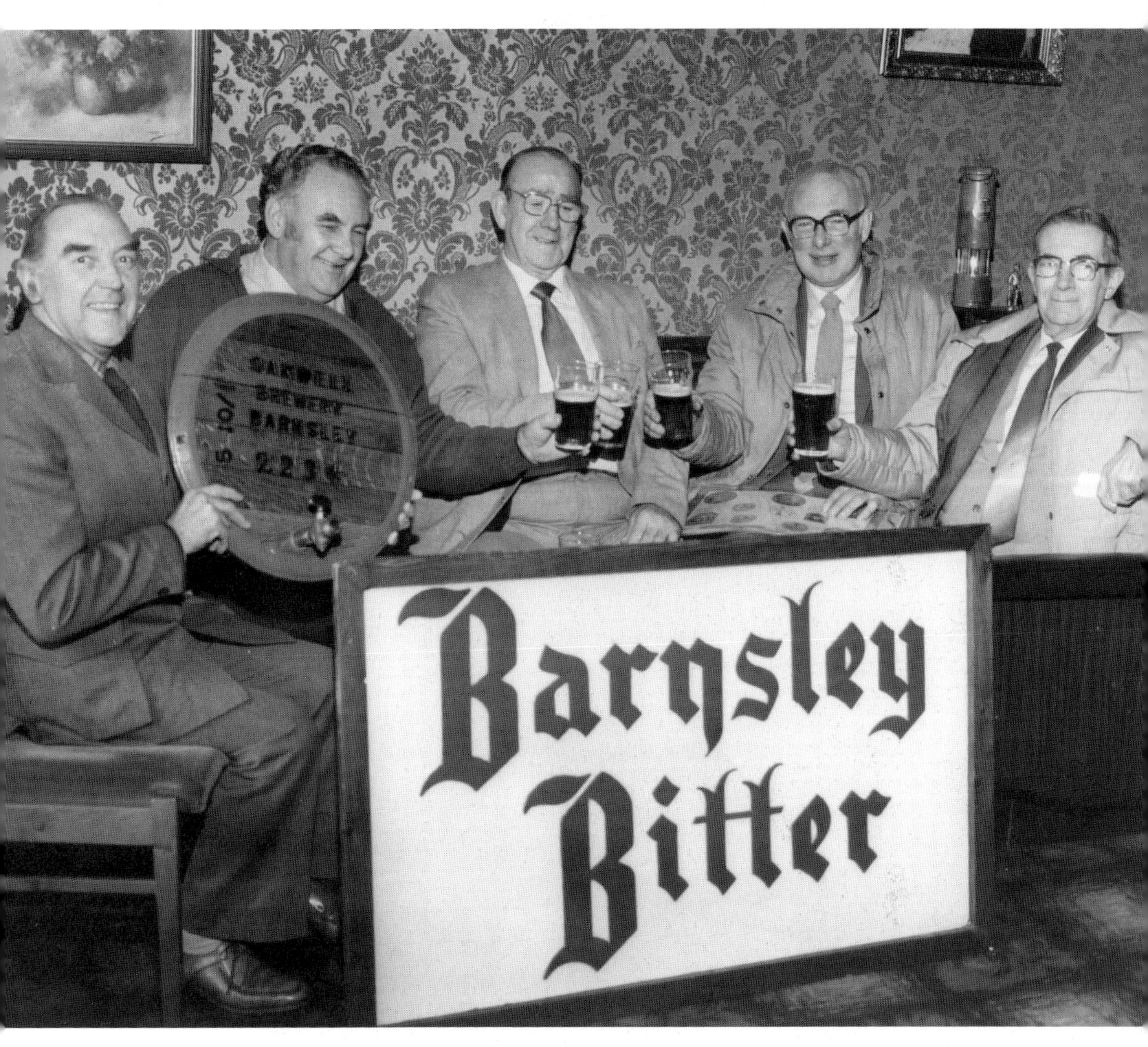

Mason with a group former brewery dreymen (seated left to right): Norman Jepson, Harold Dingle, Horace Wright and Ken Voisin, during the anti-closure campaign. (Barnsley Chronicle)

The last brewing of Oakwell Ales, in 1976, was a sad loss to the town and the once familiar delivery of Barnsley Bitter barrels has become a distant memory. (BEC)

By late 1973 the miners had slipped from number 1 in the industrial wages league to 18 and had started an overtime ban. Speaking at Mexborough, Mason, the new chairman of the miners' group of MPs, warned of 'the gravest crises of all time'. Prime Minister Heath called an election on the 'who governs Britain?' theme and the miners went on strike two days' later, 9 February 1974. Peaceful pickets such as this Yorkshire example predominated in the wake of the restrictive Industrial Relations Act. (BEC)

Part Six

Secretary of State for Defence

The Second Wilson Government, 1974-76
The Callaghan Government, 1976

'...I had to get on with with the sheer slog of... the most far-reaching review of our defences ever conducted in peacetime.'

A typical cartoon relating to Defence cuts by the notable caricaturist John Jenson, presented to Mason following its publication in the *Sunday Telegraph*, 23 March 1975. (MCA/Jenson/Sunday Telegraph)

Life and Times

1974 [5.3] Wilson appoints Mason as Secretary of State for Defence, one of the most senior cabinet posts in the new administration.

[5.3] Miners return to work.

[9.3] Five-day working week resumed.

[1.4] Reorganisation of local government.

[24.4] Mason's speech to mineworkers at Newcastle-under-Lyme in which he mentions Northern Ireland 'troops withdrawal' provokes a huge political uproar.

[9.4] Mason confirms in Parliament that the future of the Holy Loch (Scotland) Polaris base must be seen in the context of any multinational discussions.

[5] Labour's NEC working party on defence expenditure and arms exports established.
Mason addresses Council of Europe.

[19.5] State of Emergency in Northern Ireland following car bombs in Dublin and Monaghan which left 28 dead and many injured.

[1.6] An explosion at the Nypro chemical works, near Scunthorpe, kills 28 people.

[17.6] IRA bomb wrecks Westminster Hall.

[24.6] Labour Government admits Britain carried out an underground nuclear test in the Nevada desert, USA 'several weeks ago', and enrages left-wing Tribune MPs.

[26.6] 'Social Contract' agreed between Labour Government and the TUC.

[20.7] Crisis in Cyprus: Turkish invasion of the island.

[8.8] Watergate: US President Richard Nixon announces his resignation, therefore escaping impeachment.

[15.8] Mason summoned from holiday due to Cyprus crisis and oversees largest evacuation of civilians since Dunkirk.

[1-9.10] Mason 'ignores' proposed withdrawel of US Polaris bases in Britain in local election campaigning although it is mentioned in the Labour manifesto; visits aircraft carrier *Ark Royal*; prior business conduct of Lord Brayley, Mason's Parliamentary Under-Secretary for the Army in the Lords, under scrutiny and he resigns.

[10.10] General Election, the second in seven months, Labour win an overall majority of only 3 seats. Mason is returned as MP for Barnsley for the seventh time, with a 24,812 majority. He continues as Defence Secretary.

[15.10] Mason at odds with Foreign Secretary Jim Callagahan and the Left over joint Navy exercises with South Africa.

[21.11] Birmingham pub bombings, 21 killed.

[11] Mason's proposals for the Royal Yacht *Britannia* not to be retained was overruled by Harold Wilson, the Cabinet and the Chief of Defence Staff, Sir Michael Carver.

[3.12] Mason announces defence cut proposals of £4,700 million over ten

years, and reduces forces east of Suez.
RAF least affected, with Tornado project and the development of the Harrier Jump Jet to continue.
Labour MPs vote with the Tories against the Defence Review.

1975 [11.2] Margaret Thatcher is new Tory leader.
[13.2] Miners accept a 35% pay rise.
[18.3] Wilson suspends 'collective cabinet responsibity' until referendum on keeping Britain in the Common Market.
[4] Chancellor Healey demands a further £200m cut in defence budget, later revised to £110m by Wilson.
[24.4] Unemployment reaches over one million.
[4-6] Mason campaigns in favour of the Common Market.
[25.6] Mason and other pro-Europe NUM-sponsored MPs 'censored' by Yorkshire Miners' Council.
[26.6] Speaker of the House of Commons, Selwyn Lloyd, considers a 'breach of privilege' situation if sponsored MPs were instructed to vote in a particular way; Joe Gormley, NUM President, issues statement to effect that NUM would not interfere with freedom of action of its sponsored MPs.
[6.6] Referendum on Common Market: over 62% in favour of continued membership.
[15.5] Mason announces that the Royal Navy is to acquire 24 Sea Harrier jets.
[12.6] Houghton Main pit disaster, near Barnsley, 5 killed.
[24.7] Unemployment now 1.4 million, the highest since 1940.
[21.10] Mason confirms Polaris as an 'effective deterrent' in Commons speech; and takes control of the secret 'Chevaline' upgrade.
[5.12] Further defence cuts achieved from underspends and 'slippages'.
[10.12] First shots fired in the Cod War.

1976 [4.1] Five SDLP Catholics killed in an ambush by Royalist terrorists in Armagh.
[5.1.] Ten Protestant workmen are killed in a minibus ambush.
[7.1] First SAS units go to 'bandit country' of South Armagh following Mason's recommendation.
[2-3] Mason, despite a cabinet row, achieves go ahead for a Queen's Silver Jubilee medal to be struck for the armed forces.
[2.2] National Exhibition Centre opens in Birmingham.
[24.2] Royal Navy sends a fourth gun boat to Iceland.
[1.3] Northern Ireland: Merlyn Reece ends Special Category Status for scheduled terrorist crimes concerning civil violence.
[4.3] Northern Ireland under direct rule via British Parliament.
[16.3] Harold Wilson announces resignation as Prime Minister and meets the press in a room at the Ministry of Defence.
[18.3] Mason rules himself out of leadership contest despite support from

several colleagues.
[5.4] James Callaghan is new Prime Minister.
[4.] Despite all Mason's campaigning, the last beer is brewed at Barnsley's Oakwell brewery.
[5] Mason on official visit to Hong Kong, with his PPS Pat Duffy.

Overview

For Mason, his appointment as Secretary of State for Defence really was 'like coming home'. It was an area where he already had considerable expertise, after all he was a former departmental minister and had travelled widely. His manner, after formally accepting in Downing Street was described as 'ebullient' by Wilson's Policy Unit and 'kitchen cabinet' member advisor Bernard Donaghue (Donaghue, 55), though Mason recalled that Wilson warned him that the job would be 'tough'. Tough it was. The greatest challenge was dealing with the cuts in military spending, promised in Labour's Manifesto and a resolution passed with overwhelming support at the previous party conference. He was certainly aware that many party members and vocal left-wing MPs such as Frank Allaun wanted substantial cuts as well as the abandonment of Britain's nuclear deterrent. According to Barbara Castle, Allaun's attempt to get the words 'of £1,000 million' in the defence cuts floundered following 'a passionate speech by Roy Mason' who said that he was 'engaged in the most searching defence review in our history' (Castle, 183). But arguments for military savings were considerable given the poor shape of the economy and Chancellor Denis Healey's demands for public spending cuts. Mason felt that the challenge was to honour Labour's promises but at the same time maintain an effective membership of NATO. His team, consisting of Bill Rodgers (Defence Minister), Frank Judd (Navy), Bob Brown (Army) and Brynmor John (RAF); with Desmond Brayley in the Lords, had their work cut out in the weeks after the election.

Another early problem was dealing with a previously agreed sale of arms to the right-wing government of Chile, reporting to the Cabinet on 28 March 1974 that a change of policy would make Britain appear very 'unreliable' (Benn,2, 130). Later, in July 1975, he refused several Labour MPs' requests to stop training Chilean naval officers.

Defence matters took a back seat for a short but uncomfortable time following a speech to mineworkers at Newcastle-under-Lyme when Mason dared to speak frankly about Northern Ireland, saying 'Pressure is mounting on the mainland to pull out the troops'; implying that this might happen if Ulster people did not do more themselves to combat terrorism. The political reaction was immediate. His speech was the first item of business in the cabinet meeting of 25 April 1974. According to Tony Benn Harold Wilson emphasised that 'Ministers must consult with the Foreign Office, and in particular the Northern Ireland Secretary (Merlyn Reece) before saying anything' (Benn, 2, 142). Reece was 'furious' according to Barbara Castle (Castle, 89), who referred to Mason on her 'secret' diary as 'that india-rubber little man', who had not cleared his speech via the Ireland office. Benn wrote that Reece was 'desperately worried' about the situation and Belfast West MP Gerry Fitt, Leader of the Social Democratic and Labour Party (SDP) 'was furious at Roy's speech' (Benn, 2, 142).

Mason even received an embarrassing supporting letter from Sinn Fein. Despite a subsequent statement by Mason, the political damage was done, a lesson painfully experienced.

Mason could be both persuasive and determined in Cabinet meetings when speaking on a subject in which he had special interest. On 23 May 1974, for example, he made what Tony Benn described as 'a powerful speech' in favour of the Concorde project, against the likes of Roy Jenkins, Reg Prentice and Denis Healey (Benn, 2, 160).

Another 'distraction' at this time was the crisis in Cyprus involving Greek and Turkish conflicts of interest, Mason summoned from holiday to meet Wilson, Callaghan and Chiefs of Staff via the government's co-ordinating body known as COBR[A] (Cabinet Office Briefing Rooms), duly activated because of the emergency. One outcome was a mass air and sea evacuation of thousands of civilians. The situation in Cyprus, where Britain had considerable military and civilian interests, underlined Mason's case for keeping strong strategic capabilities.

Then there was another general election, the second in a year (1974). Now 50, Mason campaigned with his usual vigour, promising to use his authority in order to 'reduce defence spending and divert resources to social welfare and productive industry'. He had always supported a strong nuclear deterrent so was despondent at Labour's election manifesto pledge to 'seek the removal of American Polaris bases from Britain'. 'This was,' he later said, 'Labour at its reckless worst, swayed...by the unilateralists, the Bevanite rump, the anti-Americans and the apologists for Soviet Communism.' Polaris did not figure in his electioneering! The government and Mason in particular came under fire from left wing Labour MPs such as Ian Mikardo, the new chairman of the Parliamentary Labour Party, and Frank Allaun; and via both the Tribune Group and Labour Action for Peace. The resignation of Mason's Parliamentary Under-Secretary in the Lords, Desmond Brayley, after concerns raised in parliament about financial malpractice, was not good news shortly before election day. In Barnsley the Conservative and Liberal candidates obtained just over 18,000 votes between them but Mason still managed to attract 34,212 from an understandably lower turnout. Nationally, the situation could not have been tighter, with Labour's overall majority a precarious 3 seats.

Mason found himself at the centre of yet another political row shortly after the election. Naval exercises with South Africa Navy vessels, although in line with the Simonstown Agreement, raised a flurry of angry comments and questions from the left wing of the Party in the context of apartheid, their wrath no doubt enflamed by an endorsement of Mason's 'actions' from the chairman of the Monday Club, the right wing Conservative MP John Biggs-Davison. It was a rare occasion when Mason had a major disagreement with the Foreign Secretary, Jim Callaghan, following a 'Who runs the Navy?' banner headline in the *Evening Standard*. Callaghan was 'furious with Roy Mason' in the Cabinet meeting of 24 October 1974, according to Tony Benn (Benn, 2, 246). The Foreign Office subsequently issued a statement that the reports about the joint exercises were due to a 'verbal misunderstanding', information having not been passed on to the Foreign Secretary via our Charge d'Affairs in South Africa. Seventies spin perhaps, though interestingly Benn also recalls that 'all the manoeuvres in South Africa had been agreed between Bill Rodgers and Roy Hattersley at the Foreign Office, claiming that they were operating under a decision of the Overseas Policy Committee on 17 July' (Benn, 2, 246).

Now complete, Mason announced his Defence Review in the Commons on 3 December 1974. A 1% reduction in the proportion of defence in GNP over ten years was a substantial cut. But Britain still remained a key member of NATO, with its nuclear deterrent intact, although the Army and Navy suffered considerable reductions in equipment. The RAF was less hard hit, Mason taking great pride in keeping the Harrier jet fighter project in development. One economy that Mason failed to get the support of cabinet concerned his proposed decommissioning of the Royal Yacht *Britannia* whose considerable expense fell on the MoD. Even his suggestion that its two main users (the Foreign Office and the Board of Trade) should contribute to the running costs was turned down. In the subsequent Defence Review vote, 58 Labour MPs, led by the Tribune Group, voted against the government.

In Cabinet on 9 December 1975 Mason, according to Tony Benn, argued that he could not accept further defence cuts as it would 'appal the Germans and the Americans, break up NATO, break the Brussels Treaty and lose confidence of the Shah' (Benn,2, 476). However, defence cuts continued to be discussed in Cabinet and in the Cabinet Defence Committee during the Spring of 1975. Defence was part of a deepening economic crisis, ministers fighting in their own corner. Teamwork was not apparent: 'They leave defence to Roy Mason and the Chancellor [Denis Healey].' (Donaghue, 324). Chancellor Healey demanded defence cuts of £200M and was initially supported by Wilson. Mason refused to budge, at least regarding such a large deduction, offering £100m and gaining the support of James Callaghan, Harold Lever, Roy Jenkins and Fred Peart; and even threatened resignation. In her diaries, Barbara Castle states that Mason 'fought like a tiger' (Castle, 360), only agreeing an increase to £110 million. In May, still fighting, Mason put the case for the development of a sea-based Harrier jump jet aircraft, and subsequently endorsed by Field Marshal Carver who wanted the sea Harrier to combat the introduction of the Russian Bear reconnaissance aircraft in 1982. Cleverly, he also emphasised the importance of the Harrier as it would mean much needed employment via the aircraft industry, and trade prospects if the Shah of Iran purchased a British carrier with jump jets. Mason got the support he needed, a considerable achievement in the circumstances. It was to be against Argentina, seven years later, rather than with the Soviet Union, that the Sea Harrier proved its strategic importance.

By the autumn of 1975 when public expenditure became critical Healey was demanding defence cuts of £450 million in order to meet his £3.5 billion target. Castle described how Mason 'took the floor with a ferocious fluency that would have thought would have flattened Denis [Healey]' and warned about the possible break-up of NATO, his arguments supported by Jim Callaghan (Castle, 596/7). It is worth remembering that at the time Mason was dealing with the difficult dispute with Iceland over trawler fishing amid public and press demands for military action (which he felt was inappropriate) and was 'breathing fire' regarding Healy's demands (Donaghue, 561). Busy with the 'Cod war', Mason sent a telegram, again threatening to resign. The subject of defence spending rumbled on through to January 1976. Healey eventually reached his target but Mason's contribution, supported by Callaghan and others, amounted to £193 million, which in reality meant very little reduction as most of it was absorbed through underspending and 'slippage'. Mason's draft Defence Review 'went through on the nod' in Cabinet on 4 March 1976, according to Castle (Castle, 670), adding '- and heavens knows what hostages he has given to our fortunes'.

Mason's continued determination 'to maintain the effectiveness of the Polaris deterrent' also increased criticism in his direction from the Left of the Party and especially after Harold Wilson announced to 'an astonished Commons' (Castle, 121) in June 1974 that British nuclear testing had taken place in Nevada several weeks earlier. But the decision to upgrade Polaris had already been made, as part of the secret Chevaline project which was to stay in place until the introduction of Trident missile programme.

The spring of 1975 was notable for Mason's battle with the Left, concerning the Common Market. With the 5 June National Referendum in mind he was, as always, a staunch supporter of Europe. In the Cabinet meeting of 18 March, when a decision in favour of staying in Europe was agreed, he stressed that a withdrawal would leave Britain 'withering on the vine', adversely affecting our balance of payments and would be 'an embarrassment for the City' (Benn, 2, 348). The result confirmed his stance with 17.4 million voting 'Yes' in the referendum and 8.5 million voting 'No', a 62% majority in favour of membership. This took place against the wishes of Mason's sponsor, the NUM, and on 25 June the Yorkshire Miners' Council passed a resolution censuring Mason and other pro-European sponsored MPs. In response, a possible breach of privilege situation was raised by the Speaker of the House of Commons, Selwyn Lloyd. The matter was resolved when the NUM's President Joe Gormley stated that his union would not interfere in the freedom to vote of its sponsored MPs. Nevertheless, opposition to Mason grew from the Left in Barnsley as well as at Westminster. 'One of the things which most irritated me,' said Mason, 'was the sheer hypocrisy of many of my opponents', referring to 'colleagues' who would privately ask for help for keeping jobs in their constituencies and at the same time publicly rebuke or vote against the government on defence matters.

The escalating Troubles in Ulster also occupied a good deal of Mason's and the cabinet's time. He felt 'sick with disgust and shock' following sectarian killings on 4/5 January 1976. 'Northern Ireland was,' he said, 'like a big gas oven ready to explode' and there was serious concern that loyalist paramilitaries were 'preparing for a war footing'. In a meeting with the Prime Minister and the Northern Ireland minister, Merlyn Reece, Mason was in favour of a much stronger military presence, dispatching a 'Spearhead' battalion immediately, closing the border and suggested sending in the SAS. Wilson supported the essence of Mason's proposals, ordering a covert SAS unit into South Armagh and closing the border at a few checkpoints.

The Secretary of State for Defence may have lost the argument for the scrapping of *Britannia* (Tony Blair's Labour Government who took the final decision to decommission the Royal Yacht which sailed for the last time in 1997 and is now moored as a visitor attraction in Edinburgh's historic port of Leith) but he was always a tenacious fighter for any local or national issue in which he had strong views. A typical example occurred during the 1976 economic crisis when, on financial grounds, the Cabinet almost ditched the issue of the Queen's Silver Jubilee Medal. Mason fought hard for its retention, however, amid considerable cabinet opposition, notably from a highly critical Home Secretary, Roy Jenkins. Consequently, Harold Wilson asked the cabinet sub-committee to reappraise its costings (they had recommended abandonment). Following a further presentation by Mason, a decision was made to go ahead with the medal. Thirty thousand jubilee medals were issued to the armed forces and selected civilians in celebration of the Queen's Silver Jubilee in June 1977.

Mason was sitting directly across from Harold Wilson in cabinet on 16 March 1976 when the latter announced his resignation through a prepared statement. In his memoirs, Mason recalled the momentous occasion: 'When he had finished his statement I could see the expressions all along the other side of the table. They reflected what I felt. Shock, disappointment and surprise. Some were misty-eyed.' Apparently, Wilson spoke in a 'very matter-of-fact way' and then went on to give reasons for his decision. His rationale included statistics concerning his 'thirteen exciting and turbulent years' as leader of the Labour Party and his 31 years in Parliament, mostly on the front bench', also mentioning his great work load, seven days a week, 12-14 hours a day. Still only 60, Wilson was probably worn out by the accumulated pressure of work. Although the announcement was 'sudden' it was a retirement that he had planned at least two years earlier, had been the subject of a great deal of media speculation and was known about by several senior colleagues. But it was still a great shock. In the Commons, Edward Heath, no longer a party leader, said, of Wilson: 'Any man who has been able to lead his party successfully as you have for thirteen years, to be Prime Minister for eight years, having won four general elections, deserves the fullest tributes for his achievement'. Wilson's farewell press conference took place at the Ministry of Defence on 16 March.

Mason received some encouragement from several colleagues to stand in the new leadership election but declined, placing his support behind Jim Callagahan whose campaign was well advanced. Harold Wilson sent Mason a note, stating 'Have more courage next time'. Wilson and Mason were to remain lifelong friends.

On Callaghan's accession Mason continued in his role as Secretary of State for Defence and soon found himself on an official visit to Hong Kong, accompanied by his PPS, Patrick Duffy.

In parliament Mason denounced the new Conservative leader Margaret Thatcher, referring to her as a 'reactionary imperialist dreamer' following her attacks on the Soviet Union. He challenged the Russians to tear down the Berlin Wall and reduce their huge stock of armaments so as to demonstrate the real meaning of détente.

In a Cabinet meeting on 11 March 1976 Mason, after referring to the 'great bitterness' in the centre of the Party, argued against Jim Callaghan's suggestion for an appeal to be made to Margaret Thatcher regarding the sterling crisis, saying that support from her would not be forthcoming (Benn, 2, 530).

It was while packing his bags at home in Barnsley, prior to an important visit to the United Sates, that Mason received the most momentous telephone call of his personal and political life. Callagahan wanted him for Northern Ireland, replacing Merlyn Reece, in the most challenging job in the most challenging times imaginable.

Roy Mason, pipe in hand, looks on as the Tory candidate, a young-looking George England, signs his nomination paper in Barnsley Town Hall, 18 February 1974, ten days prior to the general election. England got almost 15,000 votes but Mason achieved well over 40,000. The person on the left is local councillor Arthur Williams. (Roy Sabine)

Closure of Polaris base demanded

A Labour MP and a Scottish Nationalist, joined to urge the Government to discuss with NATO the removal of the US Polaris base from Holy Loch.

Challenging times: this headline from the *Guardian* concerned comments in the House of Commons from Labour MP Roy Hughes (Newport) and Scottish Nationalist Winifred Ewing (Moray & Nairn), who had urged that the Government should discuss with NATO and the United States the urgent removal of the Polaris base from Holy Loch. Defence Minister Mason reinforced Labour's manifesto promise to 'seek the removal of the Polaris bases' but warned of the 'multilateral discussions which will be necessary'. (The Guardian)

Mason chairing a meeting of the Defence Council early in 1974, early in his Secretarialship. This important formal body is entrusted with the defence of the UK (and its overseas territories), accountable to the Queen and Parliament, its business facilitated via the three service boards (Admiralty, Army and Air Force). Mason is seated to the right of Bill Rodgers (Minister of State for Defence) and left of Sir Michael Carey . Sitting directly opposite Mason, fourth from the left side of the table is Lord Brayley, Under-Secretary of State for Defence (Army) whose shock resignation occurred just before the October 1974 general election. (MA)

Ulster 'must do more to end strife'

Mason lights a fuse on troop pull-out

Mason got into hot water early in his new job when he dared to mention a possible troop withdrawal from Ulster, when addressing an audience of miners at Newcastle-under-Lyme. The headline is from the *Guardian* of 25 April but the Cummings cartoon sums up the controversy perfectly. 'On Northern Ireland matters', Mason reflected later, 'careless talk can be dangerous'. (MA/The Guardian)

5 May 1974 and back in control: Mason in the cockpit of a Jaguar jet fighter at RAF Lossiemouth (Moray, Scotland), Wing Commander Terry Carlton, in charge of No 54 Squadron, looking on. The Jaguar was the RAF Strike Command's latest weapon. Today, Lossiemouth remains the largest and busiest RAF base for fast-jet aircraft. (MA)

Mason addresses the Council of Europe during its 25th anniversary celebrations, Strasbourg, 6-10 May 1974. (Council of Europe)

24 June 1974: Defence Secretary Mason and the Labour Government came under a barrage of criticism, particularly from the left-wing Tribune Group and Labour Action for Peace, when news of an a British underground nuclear test in Nevada, USA (originally arranged by the previous Conservative Government), was released. Frank Allaun (seen here) warned of 'the grave danger' of the bomb spreading to more countries, preferring 'suicide missiles' to be scrapped. Mason emphasised that there was no party commitment to abolish nuclear weapons, nor had the government broken any international agreements. It would be like abandoning our strategic deterrent - 'and that's not on,' he said. (MA)

Yet another general election. Mason is pictured outside Barnsley Town Hall with the two other candidates: Liberal P Tomlinson (left) and, once again, for the Conservatives, local barrister George England, 30 September 1974. (Roy Sabine)

ROY MASON

Who is 50 years of age, married with two children

HAS served you for the past 21 years in Westminster.
HIS record during that time is well known to you all.
HAS served his Country as Postmaster General — Minister of Power — President of the Board of Trade and Secretary of State for Defence.
HAS continued to champion the cause of his constituents including the Miners; until recently was Chairman of the Miners' Group and the Labour Group of Yorkshire M.P.s.
CONTINUED by conscientious attendance, his Town Hall Bureau, through which thousands of constituents have sought his advice and assistance.
HAS personally pioneered schemes to help Pensioners and the Disabled.
NATIONALLY recognised — LOCALLY respected and admired.

THIS IS YOUR MAN

Renew your Confidence
by VOTING FOR
ROY MASON
Thursday, 10th October, 1974.
Hours of Poll — 7 a.m. to 10 p.m.

You will receive direct from the Returning Officer a card giving your Poll Number and telling you where to VOTE.
If you spoil your Ballot Paper don't hesitate to ask for another one.

Published by J. L. Hammill, "Karinya", 28 Issott Street, Barnsley.
Printed by Chronicle Printers, Church Street, Barnsley.

Extract from Mason's election leaflet. In speeches his main theme concerned reducing defence spending so that resources could be diverted to 'social welfare and productive industry'. (MA)

Surrounded by a sea of Barnsley school children, a few days before the general election, 4 October 1974. Understandably, the turn out was down on February (by 6.2%) but Mason still managed to poll over 34,000 votes, obtaining a substantial Labour majority of 24,812. (MA)

The Labour Front Bench, October 1974, Mason sat between Tony Benn and Barbara Castle. The full line-up, left to right, is: Robert Mellish (Chief Whip), Roy Jenkins (Home Secretary), James Callaghan (Foreign Secretary), Harold Wilson (Prime Minister), Denis Healey (Chancellor of the Exchequer), Peter Shore (Trade), Tony Benn (Industry), Roy Mason (Defence), Barbara Castle (Health & Social Security), Fred Peart (Agriculture, Fisheries & Food) and John Silkin (Planning and Local Government). (MA)

An alternative interpretation of Labour's Front Bench, presented to Mason by the cartoonist Richard Wilson. Featured, left to right, are: Peter Shore, Anthony Crosland, Edward Short, Roy Jenkins, Harold Lever, Tony Benn, Shirley Williams, Denis Healey, Harold Wilson, James Callaghan, Barbara Castle and Roy Mason. Just behind Callaghan and Wilson are Michael Foot and Reg Prentice. The Opposition Bench includes the umistakable profile of Edward Heath. (MCA/R Wilson)

Left fires first salvo at South Africa sea trials

Typical headline following Royal Navy exercises with South Africa's maritime forces. The event was a legitimate part of the Simonstown Agreement but for Mason and his Navy minister, Frank Judd, it resulted in another barrage of criticism from left-wing Labour colleagues such as Bob Cryer, speaking in the context of the apartheid policies of the Republic. Mason was quick to point out in the corridors of Westminster that the exercises had in fact taken place via the Foreign Office and our Charge Affairs in South Africa - rather than the MoD. (The Guardian)

Mason receiving HRH Prince Charles at the RAF Aircraft Museum, Colindale, north London, 4 December 1975. It concerned the opening of an exhibition, 'Wings of the Eagle', devoted to the history of German aviation. It was housed in a new extension to the Museum, named the Dermot Boyle Wing, after its founding Chairman of Trustees, Marshal of the Air Force Sir Dermot Boyle. His Royal Highness opened both the exhibition and the new extension. The Museum itself, on the site of the old London Aerodrome, was opened by HM the Queen three years earlier. (MA)

.R. - 2 -

for a modern and effective defence structure and will make a significant contribution to establishing our economic health and thus to strengthening the Alliance.

3. The Government has decided that it should reduce defence expenditure as a proportion of GNP from its present level of 5½ per cent to 4½ per cent over the next ten years. The long range estimates of defence expenditure as they stood in March 1974 would have amounted to 6 per cent of GNP in 1978-9 and 5½ per cent in 1983-4. By comparison with those plans, our decision will save £300 million in 1975-6, about £500 million a year by 1978-9, and some £750 million a year by 1983-4 - or a total over the whole period up to that date of about £4,700 million. This is fully consistent with our repeated pledges to reduce the cost of defence as a proportion of our national resources.

4. In addition to deciding the general scale of the programme needed to meet our future defence requirements and the level of resources we can devote to defence, the Government has reached provisional

/ conclusions ...

This is page 2 of Mason's actual speech in the House of Commons in which he announced his Defence Review, 3 December 1974. The verso page includes hand-written notes made either last minute or after the presentation. 58 Labour MPs 'who habitually used the word "comrade"(Mason's words)... marched into the lobbies against the government.' (MA)

The witty pen of Leslie Illingworth (1902-79), concerning Mason and the defence cuts. (MCA/Leslie Illingworth/News of the World)

This cartoon presented to Roy Mason by Emmwood (John Musgrave-Wood, 1915-99), is titled 'Raw Recruit' and shows a dishevelled 'Private Mason' perspiring under the onslaught of a loud Drill Sergeant. (MCA/ J Musgrave-Wood/Daily Mail)

Suitably dressed when visiting Northern Ireland as Defence Secretary in 1975, his ever present protection officer in the background. (MA)

Marjorie and Roy Mason walking behind ex-Premier Harold Macmillan by the lawns at the front of the Ministry of Defence, on their way to the unveiling of a statue (created by Oscar Neman) to the late Lord Portal of Hungerford (Sir Charles Frederick Algernon Portal, 1893-1971), former Marshal of the Royal Air Force and British Chief of the Air Staff during most of the Second World War. The ceremony, led by Macmillan, took place in 1975. (MA)

The Wilson Cabinet (c.1975). Seated (left to right) are: Shirley Williams, Michael Foot, Denis Healey, Lord Elwyn Jones, Edward Short, Harold Wilson, Jim Callaghan, Roy Jenkins, Anthony Crosland, Tony Benn and Barbara Castle. Standing are (left to right): Fred Mulley, Robert Mellish, Harold Lever, Merlyn Reece, William Ross, Peter Shore, Eric Varley, Roy Mason, John Morris, Fred Peart, Lord (Malcom) Shepherd, Reginald Prentice, and John Silkin. (MA)

In the Palace Garden, Muscat with His Imperial Majesty Qaboos bin Sa'id al Said, the new Sultan of Oman who had ascended to power in July 1970, succeeding his exiled father. Privately educated in Britain, the Sultan had served as an officer in the British Army after graduating from the Royal Military Academy, Sandhurst. The head of a key Gulf state, his reign was actively supported by British governments, so Mason's visit was an important one. Qaboos remains as the 14th descendant of the Al Bu Sai'd dynasty but has no direct heir. (MA)

Mason was tireless in his support for the Harrier Jump Jet and in 1975 managed to secure for an appreciative Royal Navy an order for 25 of its maritime version, the Sea Harrier. 'There is no doubt', said Mason 'that the maritime Harrier will substantially improve the effectiveness and capability of our anti-submarine task forces.' Following the Cabinet meeting in which development approval was given, Mason and his PPS Patrick Duffy, the Sheffield Attercliffe MP, visited RAF Cotteshall and celebrated by flights in land Harriers to Brough, on Humberside, where major work on the seagoing version was to be undertaken. A large plaque with the legend 'WELCOME AND THANK YOU MR MASON' greeted them on landing. The Sea Harrier's considerable capabilities came to the fore during the subsequent Falklands conflict. (MA)

In Waterdale, Doncaster, pictured on a dias in the car park, ready to take the salute alongside Air Marshal Sir Neville Stack (on Mason's left), Wing Commander Mike Burton and the Mayor, Councillor Gerry McDade, on Sunday 12 October 1975. The occasion was the granting of the Freedom of Entry into the new metropolitan borough (its highest civic honour) on RAF Finningley. (MA)

After the ceremony a support squadron from RAF Finningley marched to the Mansion House where the Mayor of Doncaster took the salute on a packed pavement. The Finningley base was decommissioned 21 years later, in 1996, and since 2005 has functioned as an international airport (Robin Hood Doncaster Sheffield). (MA)

Although watered down, the further defence cuts announced early in the New Year (1976) resulted in media criticism, especially from the more right-wing newspapers. The *Daily Express* cartoonist, Leeds-born Arthur Cummings, portrayed Mason as 'Minister of Defenceless', placing him at the top of Nelson's column, a placard attached to his reversed telescope proclaiming 'I see no Red Fleet!', 28 January 1976. (MCA/Cummings/Daily Express)

HM the Queen was given a tremendous reception when she visited Barnsley in 1975, seen here on Cheapside. Two years later Silver Jubilee street partie took place all over Britain but there had been a row i the Cabinet during the 1976 economic crisis over the financing and issue of a jubilee medal. It was largely Mason's stubborn persistence via the MoD that resulted in Harold Wilson requesting more accurate costings rather than abandoning the traditional commemorative issue. After Wilson's resignation Jim Callaghan's new cabinet approved the issue of 30,000 jubilee medals, principally for the armed forces but also for selected civilians. (Sheffield newspapers/BEC)

The Callaghan Cabinet as it was in April 1976. For this montage Mason obtained the signatures of all the members. (MA)

In May 1976 Mason embarked on an an official visit to Hong Kong, accompanied by his PPS, Patrick Duffy. Like Mason, Duffy was a pro-European and opposed unilateral nuclear disarmament. It was towards the end of this visit that Duffy received news of his appointment by Callaghan as Under-Secretary of State for the Navy. A distinguished former pilot in the Fleet Air Arm during World War Two, Duffy became a good friend of the Masons. The photographs shows Mason being welcomed after embarking from the RAF aircraft, Marjorie just behind him and Duffy carrying a brief case. (MA)

Facing the press during Mason's official visit to Hong Kong. (MA)

Inspecting troops shortly after arrival in Hong Kong. (MA)

One of his last duties as Defence Secretary: welcoming HM The Queen when she arrived at Horse Guards to watch the Massed Bands of HM Royal Marines Beat Retreat. The latter in celebration of the birthday of its Captain General, HRH The Duke of Edinburgh, seen just behind HRH. The First Sea Lord, Admiral Sir Edward Ashmore, awaits his introduction to Her Majesty, 10 June 1976. (MA)

Part Seven

Callaghan's Call

Secretary of State for Northern Ireland 1976-79

'From the centre of Belfast...flames were leaping into the air, clouds of greasy black smoke coiling and billowing across the city...They boasted afterwards that it was Mason's baptism of fire.'

The Secretary of State for Northern Ireland was certainly in a political hot seat, transformed as per Dr Jeckyll to Mr Hyde according to his friendly cartoonist Rowel Friers for the *Irish Times*, 1977. (MCA/Rowell Friers/Irish Times)

Life and Times

1976 [1.6] Interim agreement to end 'Cod War' with Iceland.
[21.7] Christopher Ewart-Biggs, British Ambassador to the Irish Republic assassinated, Sandyford, Co. Dublin.
[7.8] Women's Peace Movement of Northern Ireland holds its first rally of 20,000 Protestants and Roman Catholics.
[9.8] Gerry Fitt, SDLP Leader, drives a Republican mob from his house at gunpoint.
[14.8] 10,000 Protestant and Catholic women demonstrate for peace in Northern Ireland.
[22/31.8] Drought is the worst in Britain since records began; Denis Howell is created 'Minister for Drought'.
[25.8] Unemployment passes 1.5 million mark.
[2.9] European Commission on Human Rights reports on Irish Government's charges against Britain: British authorities are found guilty of torturing detainees in Ulster following the introduction of internment in 1971 (but not guilty of discriminating between Protestants and Republican extremists).
[4.9] Peace march in Derry.
[10.9] Roy Mason replaces Merlyn Reece as Ulster Secretary, Reece becoming Home Secretary.
[21.10] Michael Foot is new Deputy Leader of the Labour Party.
[29.10] Mining starts in the new Selby Coalfield.
[7.11] 1,662 crosses are planted in Belfast in respect of those who have lost their lives during the Troubles in Ireland since 1969.
[27.11] Mrs Jane Ewart-Biggs, widow of the assassinated British Ambassador is one of leaders of peace march in London.
[10.12] Betty Williams and Mairead Corrigan win Nobel Peace Prize.

1977 [3.1] Roy Jenkins, former Home Secretary and Labour Deputy Leader resigns as an MP to become the first President of the EEC Commission.
[29.1] Seven IRA bombs explode in London's West End.
[4.2] IRA 'bomb factory' found in Liverpool.
[6.2] Silver Jubilee of the Queen's accession.
[10.2] IRA terrorists involved in Balcombe Street siege jailed for life, for six murders.
[21.2] Dr David Owen (38) is new Foreign Secretary.
[19.3] Margaret Thatcher says the Tories were 'ready for an election'.
[2.4] Tory Ulster spokesman Airey Neave says that Provisional Sinn Fein should be banned.
[15.4] Miners demand an end to Social Contract.
[30.4] The Rev Ian Paisley threatens to resign if the Loyalist strike call is ignored.

[1.5] Mason meets strike leaders Paisley and Baird.
Army reinforcements in Northern Ireland due to imminent Loyalist general strike, due to start at midnight.
[3.5] 'Paisley thugs' said to be intimidating non-strikers.
[16.5] IRA claims it has kidnapped, interrogated and killed a British Army officer.
[17.6] Fianna Fail win Irish general election, Jack Lynch becomes premier.
[7.6] Queen's Silver Jubilee festivities week starts.
[2.7] UM demands £135 and a four-day week for miners.
[10.8] The Queen makes an official visit to Northern Ireland as part of her Silver Jubilee celebrations.
[10.10] Betty Williams and Mairead Corrigan, founders of the Women's Peace Movement in Ulster are awarded the Nobel Peace Prize.
[3.11] Industrial action stops the televising of the state opening of Parliament.

1978 [18.1] European Court of Human Rights finds the UK government guilty of mistreating prisoners in Northern Ireland, but not guilty of torture.
[8.2] Car booby trap kills a UDR man and his daughter.
[17.2] La Mon House restaurant bombing, near Belfast, 12 killed and 30 injured.
[18.2] 20 IRA suspects arrested in response to the La Mon bombing, including Gerry Adams, a senior Provisional Sinn Fein member.
[25.2] Gerry Adams is charged with membership of the IRA.
[7.4] Callaghan meets Jack Lynch, Irish premier for 'mini-summit' on Ireland.
[10.6] Amnesty International report on ill-treatment of terrorist suspects by RUC. Mason had earlier rejected a public inquiry but announced a private investigation, on advice of Sir Kenneth Newman, into 'police practice and procedures' re RUC's alleged treatment of terrorist suspects.
[21.6] Shooting between Provisional IRA and British Army: 1 civilian and 3 IRA men killed.
[3.8] De Lorean Motor Company to build new motor plant on a 56 acre green field site near Belfast.
[9] Public service strikes start and continue into winter period.
[17.12] IRA bombs explode in Southampton, Bristol, Manchester and Coventry.
[21.12] Three soldiers shot dead in Northern Ireland

1979 [8.1] Oil tanker explodes in Bantry Bay, Ireland, 49 die.
[10.1] Industrial unrest in Britain: 'Crisis? What crisis?' (James Callaghan).
[22.1] 'Winter of Discontent' strikes, dustbins overflow and streets pile up with rubbish.
[16.3] Northern Irish prisoners have been injured in police custody according to the Bennett Report.

[28.3] The Government is defeated in a vote of confidence, and a general election is called for 3 May.
[30.3] An IRA terrorist car bomb kills Airey Neave, the Tory Ulster spokesman, in the car park at Westminster.
[17.4] 4 policemen killed by a huge IRA bomb.

Overview

It was 10 am on a Friday morning when the phone rang. Roy and Marjorie were at their Barnsley home, packing bags in preparation for an important visit to the United States. Jim Callagahan told Mason that he wanted him to be Secretary of State for Northern Ireland, part of a reshuffle. Mason accepted, after a reassuring discussion with 'his rock', Marjorie, who was supportive as ever, though well aware of the potential dangers of the job. Only weeks earlier Christopher Ewart-Biggs, British Ambassador to the Irish Republic, was killed by an IRA bomb, along with Judith Cooke, secretary to senior civil servant Brian Cubbon who was also injured. It was now a question of getting to London as soon as possible in order to discuss matters further at 10 Downing Street where Callaghan met him in the Cabinet Room.

As Defence Secretary Mason had visited the troops in Northern Ireland and was well aware of the immense difficulties that Merlyn Reece had faced during his two years in the job. For Mason, security was the priority. He believed that nothing else could be achieved unless this was constantly high profile. Next came the Northern Ireland economy, the seedbed for terrorists. New investment and jobs were vital. The Province 'needed hope where it was desperately needed'. Regarding constitutional reform, the right conditions were needed before any real progress could be made. This common sense strategy was informally agreed with Callaghan. It was a good start.

Mason was given a sound ministerial team, led by the much respected Mansfield MP Don Concannon, a former mineworker and a government whip. The junior ministers consisted of Ray Carter (Birmingham Northfield), Jimmy Dunn (Liverpool Kirkdale) and by far the youngest, the only person that Mason was not fully acquainted with, Lord Melchett.

The next day Mason, accompanied by Marjorie were at Stormont Castle, meeting civil service officials but the helicopter journey from Aldergrove was memorable. Parts of Belfast could be seen alight with fires, buses burning in the streets, 'a [Loyalist] terrorist spectacular laid on for my benefit'. Marjorie, a former Land Army girl, later recalled her immediate reaction: 'My stomach felt like it did when the sirens went off during the war.' But she also said that this was not the real Northern Ireland, a place and people that she soon grew to be very fond of, despite the Troubles.

Mason lived in Northern Ireland for almost three years, clocking up a huge mileage of air travel, only returning to London for Cabinet meetings. Marjorie usually joined him every fortnight, taking part in a variety of non-political and charity events. For Roy, much of the Province reminded him of his native Yorkshire, having its own distinctive flavour' independent, proud and fiercely patriotic.' He enjoyed the landscape and scenery too, 'with its many shades of green' saying that 'its sheer beauty envelopes you and gives you a sense of warmth and contentment - peace - and most of Northern Ireland is at peace and peaceful - trouble spots are only spots'. For leisure there was nothing to surpass walking in the hills or a few hours fishing, even though the protection officers were ever present.

At Mason's first press conference he emphasised that he wanted to revive the Northern Ireland economy 'ruined by violent gangsterism'. Factories had been destroyed and thousands of families uprooted because of violence or intimidation and unemployment was 11.4%. His pronouncement was reviewed on 10 October by the Belfast correspondent of the Observer, Andrew Stephen, under the headline 'Mason's hard choice'. His 'pugnaciously confident' message that 'the Provisional IRA is reeling, the security forces are winning the fight against terrorism and that ordinary people are rejecting the bombers and gunmen', was 'predictable', though Stephen concluded that 'whatever choice the British Government makes, it will be mightily unpopular in one quarter or another.' There would be some criticism for anything he did.

Central to Mason's policies in Northern Ireland (and following on from Merlyn Reece's decision to end 'special category status' after 1 March 1976) was that convicted terrorists, irrespective of their religious and political backgrounds, should be treated as criminals rather than political prisoners. He had a burgeoning problem dealing with developments at the former RAF station at Long Kesh, near Lisburn, where the H-Blocks of the Maze prison, used to house those convicted of scheduled terrorist offences, were located. Characteristically, Mason stood firm against the so-called 'on the blanket' protest whereby inmates refused to work, wear prison uniforms and wrapped themselves in bedsheets. The situation escalated into the 'dirty protest', many prisoners smearing excrement on the walls of their cells. 'Whatever happened, I was determined not to budge,' recalled Mason. 'The prisoners were criminals and as far as I was concerned would always be treated as criminals.' Fuelled by media reports, the 'dirty strike' resulted in a wave of criticism from a variety of individuals and organisations. These included Lord Brockway and the Howard League for Penal Reform, the National Council for Civil Liberties and Amnesty International. The Peace People, gained the support of the Bishop of Derry and called for 'emergency status' for the prisoners. Statistics reported to Parliament by Don Concannon stated that 300 H-blocks prisoners were fouling their cells, 74 of them being convicted of murderer or attempted murder and 162 of firearms offences or crimes involving explosives. However, this attempt to satisfy MPs and public received a set back at the end of July 1978 after Dr Thomas O Fiaich's, (Archbishop of Armagh and Roman Catholic Primate of All England) visit to the Maze. His comments described some of the conditions as 'unfit for animals' and that the prisoners 'would prefer death to be being classified as criminals'.

Mason admits mixed success in his relations with some of the key political figures in Northern Ireland. The hardest by far to communicate with was the DUP (Democratic Unionist Party) leader and North Antrim MP, Reverend Ian Paisley, described by political journalist John Cole in an *Observer* profile (8 May 1977) as 'the most anachronistic figure in modern public life' at the time of the Loyalist strike. Mason saw him as 'domineering', and found it hard to 'warm to the man' but 'respected his dedication as constituency MP'. For the Nationalists, Mason regarded the Foyle MP John Hume of the SDLP (Social Democratic and Labour Party) as 'politically astute' and 'was genuinely working for his people', though he did find it difficult to contact him. Although generally regarded in Westminster as 'genial and warm-hearted' Mason's relations with the SDLP leader, Gerry Fitt, were never good. But he always respected his honesty, sincerity and great courage, especially when he refused to support the dirty strike protesters. Relations were far better with Oliver Napier, the Alliance Party leader 'a good man, representing a good cause'.

The greatest threat to complete civil unrest in Northern Ireland, according to Mason, came in the spring of 1977. It was not the actions of the IRA but the United Ulster Action (UUAC) strike, led by the DUP leader, Reverend Ian Paisley, and his ally, Ernest Baird. With 1974 a recent memory, Mason was determined that the 'Paisley strike' would fail. On 30 April, a few days before the strike began, Paisley made his much-reported statement that he would quit politics if the strike was not supported. John Cole, writing a profile of Paisley under the headline 'Ulster's Holy Terror' in the *Observer* of 8 May, remarked that the DUP leader's announcement 'contained enough small print to give a man of his intellectual suppleness a way out of that threat (or promise) if he wants one'. Cole concluded that Paisley was 'more proficient at expressing hatred and contempt than friendship and kindness,' saying that he was 'a dangerous man'. Mason regarded 'bombastic' Paisley as a supporter of 'balaclava-clad bullies' who were 'creating fear and tension in the Province'. He took personal control of the strike from his Stormont Castle office and had the Army on stand by to seize the power stations and was prepared to declare a state of emergency in case draconic powers were needed. When Paisley turned up for one meeting with Mason fifteen minutes late he was told in no uncertain terms by the blunt Yorkshireman that his time was up after 15 minutes of his previously allotted 30 minute interview. But Mason's diplomacy and pugnacious approach kept most of the power workers from joining the strike. Intimidation was widespread after the strike began on 3 May and though bus driver Harry Bradshaw was shot dead most people went to work as normal. Paisley, Baird and eleven other 'agitators' were arrested for obstruction and held for a short time though no charges were made. Despite the barricades in Ballymena town, the Province as a whole was not paralysed. By 13 May Mason was even able to take the salute at a passing-out parade of the Royal Irish Rangers in Paisley's Ballemena.

Jim Callaghan issued the following minute to the Cabinet on 17 May commending Mason's role during the crisis:

> 'You have displayed courage and firmness against these dangerous men and by your successful appeal to the good sense and loyalty of the people of Ulster you have achieved a signal victory over those whose unconstitutional actions would have destroyed the economic recovery you have done so much to promote.'

Mason considered the 'real heroes' of the confrontation were 'the ordinary men and women of Northern Ireland, people who had braved the blackmailers and the thugs...who stood up for themselves, their families and the wider community.'

On the same day that he received Callaghan's praise news reached Mason which affected him badly. Captain Robert Nairac, aged 29, a Grenadier Guardsman who had been working undercover, liaising with the SAS, was abducted from a pub in Drumintee, South Armagh on the evening of 14 May, violently interrogated by a suspicious IRA gang and killed after he refused to give out any information. Six men were subsequently convicted of murder or manslaughter and jailed. Thirty-two years after Nairac's death, in May 2008, police arrested Kevin Crilly in South Armargh and also charged him with Nairic's murder. Nairic was posthumously awarded the George Cross but his body has never been found.

A factor in the failure of the strike may have been due to the poor state of the Northern Ireland economy where unemployment was twice that of the UK. In some of the worst areas 30% of the adult male adult population was unemployed. People in work did not want to lose their jobs. Mason worked hard to encourage new investment into the Province. In Cabinet (7.12.77) he fought to save 10,000 jobs by retaining regional employment premiums when they were abolished in Britain. Ulster's expenditure cuts were reduced from £30 million to £5 million and he obtained a large order for the Belfast shipyard. Even with hindsight, Mason told me that he had no regrets about the De Lorean affair. At the time the prospect of building a new motor car factory in one of the most needy parts of Belfast was welcome news for all concerned. One journalist (Robert Rodwell, *Observer*, 6 August 1978) described him as looking like' a cat that had stolen a barrel full of cream' when the public announcement was made, describing the news as 'the biggest economic coup for more than a decade'. Mason had indeed fought hard for Cabinet approval, regarding it as a tremendous achievement, '...one of the best things I ever did,' though he also saw the resultant financial abuses of the Company as 'one of the most bitter disappointments of my life'. He remains adamant, however, that much blame should be placed on the incoming Tory administration for its lack of monitoring of the Company's spending.

Mason's working relations with the RUC (Royal Ulster Constabulary) and the Army appear to have been amicable most of the time. He found the Chief Constable, Kenneth Newman 'strict in his observance of the law and straight as a die' and a man 'of utter integrity'. Newman was newly appointed (May 1976) but had worked as Deputy Chief Constable since 1973. As a young man he served in the Palestine Police Force so was no stranger to public order problems and terrorism. For the Army, the Commanding Officer (GOC), David House, was 'totally reliable, a soldier's soldier'. Mason was also committed to improve relations between the RUC and the Army.

Faced with allegations of police brutality towards terrorist suspects following investigations by Amnesty International, Mason, on the advice of Newman, set up an inquiry into 'police practice and procedures' in 1978. Media and Northern Ireland political criticism focussed on the 'behind closed doors' nature of the response, saying that only a public inquiry would obtain the truth. 'I wasn't in the least surprised to be attacked from all sides for that decision,' said Mason. Earlier, in the summer of 1977, hundreds of terrorist suspects were held and interrogated at Castlereagh and leaked stories of ill-treatment appeared, the RUC's methods featured on a BBC *Tonight* programme. Amnesty refused Mason's request for the name of informants regarding apparent cases of brutality. The Bennett Report, published in March 1979, did find evidence of suspects being injured in police custody but also reported on 'a co-ordinated and extensive campaign to discredit the police'. Mason accepted the key recommendations of Judge Bennett, including the use of closed-circuit TVs in interrogation rooms, better access to solicitors, improved medical care and complaints procedure.

Mason had a running battle with the BBC (and to a lesser extent ITV) over its coverage of what he called 'balaclava-clad terrorists' which he felt was 'helping the propaganda campaign' of the IRA in particular. A big row occurred in 1977 following forthright remarks that he made to Lord Swann and other BBC Governors in which he criticised programming policy, showing images which he felt 'encouraged violence and undermined democracy'.

Mason experienced what he later described as 'the worst weekend of my political life' between 17-19 February 1978. On the Friday, Lieutenant-Colonel Ian Corden-Lloyd, Commander of the 2nd Battalion of the Royal Green Jackets was killed when his military helicopter crashed near the Irish border. Then, at the La Mon Hotel restaurant near Belfast, an incendiary bomb killed twelve people and injured many others. The innocent victims, apparently Protestants, were members of of the Irish Collie Club and the Northern Ireland Junior Motor Cycle Club, so included children and young persons. At the scene the next morning, Mason described the act as 'the worst act of terrorism since the Troubles began' and 'an act of criminal irresponsibility'. With his blessing, the RUC prepared a leaflet for distribution which included some images of the dreadful carnage and there was a roundup of suspects. Some Loyalists at the time blamed Mason's 'complacency' for the attack which the IRA admitted was their responsibility, stating that their 9-minute warning was inadequate.

Five weeks before the General Election, late in the afternoon of Friday 30 March 1979, news reached Mason at his Stormont office that his PPS (Parliamentary Private Secretary), Alan Williams had been killed in a terrorist attack within the precincts of Westminster. Soon the real victim and circumstances became known. Airey Neave, the Conservative Shadow Northern Ireland spokesman, and close ally of Margaret Thatcher, was a fatal victim of a bomb planted in his vehicle, exploding as he drove up the exit ramp of the Commons underground car park. It was apparently the work of the INLA (Irish National Liberation Army). It was a shocking and sickening blow as Mason knew Neave well, working with him on official bipartite and secret talks.

A recent book by Walter Ellis (Ellis, p251) suggests that Mason was the planned target for killing, the INLA's assasin switching to Neave because of the latter's weak protection compared with the Secretary of State; also, it was feared that Neave would be a very tough Secretary of State if the Tories, as seemed likely, won the impending Election. A Sinn Fein 'Stuff Mason' march the previous month had also demonstrated a dangerous level of hatred. But the Neave assassination emphasised that Mason was a high profile target for terrorist groups, and that protection at all times was essential. What the Yorkshireman did not realise at the time was that this requirement was to continue for much of the rest of his life.

And yet statistics gradually showed that the situation in Northern Ireland had improved under Mason. In 1976 1,276 people had been charged with terrorist offences (241 of them for murder or attempted murder) and there were 963 convictions. By mid 1977 only 353 suspects were charged (67 for murder/attempted murder). Deaths relating to the conflict reached 297 in 1976, falling dramatically to 112 in 1977 (Mason's first full year as Secretary of State) and only 81 the year after. Writing about statistical 'good news' in the *Observer* on 18 December 1977, John Cole described how violence had been 'cut by half this year', with four deaths for every ten killed in 1976. Speaking about Mason, he refers to him as 'no genius, but his colour blindness between orange and green is a positive virtue'.

Life in Pictures

The Northern Ireland ministerial team: (left to right) Raymond Carter, 'Don' (James Dennis) Concannon, Roy Mason, James Dunn and Lord Melchett (Peter Mond, 4th Baron Melchett). Carter, who represented Birmingham Northfield, was described by Mason as 'a workaholic with a solid background of local government...[and] utterly trustworthy...' Concannon, a former Nottinghamshire miner and NUM official, was MP for Mansfield and regarded by Mason to be 'someone I knew I could rely on when the going got rough'. Jimmy Carter, Labour Member of Parliament for Liverpool Kirkdale, was a Roman Catholic who helped the 'balance' of the team, 'and might be able to reach out to the minority community of the province'. Callaghan's surprise recommendation was Lord Melchett, only 28, and described by Mason as 'very green' because of his environmental interests, and 'not the type I'd personally chose to face the terrorists'. (MA)

The leaders of the three main political parties prepare to lay wreaths at the Cenotaph, November 1976. They are, left to right: David Steel, Margaret Thatcher and Jim Callaghan. The former Tory leader and Prime Minister, Edward Heath stands to the left of Steel, Mason is on the second row, between Thatcher and Callaghan. (MA)

The Labour Cabinet of 1978/79: (back row, left to right) Cabinet Secretary, John Smith, Bill Rodgers, John Silkin, Fred Peart, Albert Booth, John Morris, Bruce Millan, Fred Mulley, David Ennals, Joel Barnet, Roy Hattersley, Stan Orme and Harold Lever; (front row, left to right) Peter Shore, Tony Benn, Denis Healey, Michael Foot, Jim Callaghan, Elwyn Jones, Merlyn Reece, Shirley Williams, Eric Varley and Roy Mason. (MA)

Betty Williams (left) with folk singer Joan Baez and co-founder of the Community of Peace People, Mairead Corrigan (right) after a march to Trafalgar Square, 27 November 1976. Next to Mairead is Jane Ewart-Biggs, the widow of the British Ambassador (Christopher Ewart-Biggs) who had been killed by a land mine concealed in a culvert, planted by the IRA at Sandyford, Dublin, on 21 July. Judith Cooke (26), Private Secretary to Sir Brian Cubbon, Permanent Under Secretary of State (the most senior civil servant working with Mason) was also killed in the attack and both Cubbon and the car's driver, Brian O'Driscoll, were injured. Williams and Corrigan were awarded the Nobel Peace Prize in 1977 (for 1976). (MA)

Chistopher Ewart-Biggs, British Ambassador to Ireland. Aged 54 when he was killed, Ewart-Biggs was a veteran of the El Alemain (1942) where he lost his right eye. (MA)

Two photographs taken by Mason. The first is of 'Stormont', Northern Ireland Parliament Buildings (now home of the Northern Ireland Assembly), situated in the Stormont Estate, east of Belfast. The classical style building of Portland stone, opened in 1932, was to the design of the architect Sir Arnold Thornley who also got the commission for Barnsley Town Hall (1932-33), so Mason even had local connections here. A proposed 'ministerial building' was never executed, Stormont Castle serving as the Belfast office of Mason and his ministers, though for meals and accommodation use was also made of nearby Stormont House, the old Speaker's official residence. The second image shows one of the army helicopters used by Mason, at Stormont. For security reasons, especially after the Ewart-Briggs assassination, he always travelled by chopper. His first flight over Belfast was a memorable one, flames and smoke coming from the city, a deliberate 'baptism of fire' for the new Secretary of State. He was then briefed and told that the welcome was from Loyalists of the Ulster Defence Association rather than the IRA, in protest about the alleged treatment of Protestants in the Maze prison. (MA)

Hillsborough Castle, County Down, the Georgian country mansion remains the official residence of the Secretary of State for Northern Ireland and his or her junior ministers. For the Masons the place was an oasis of 'peace and tranquility' where they were able to relax on albeit guarded strolls through the grounds and to the village church on Sunday mornings. It was not until the secretarialship of Mo Mowlam (1997-99) that it was deemed safe for the grounds to be open to the public, in May and June. (MA)

Roy and Marjorie Mason (centre) with the Chief Constable of the Royal Ulster Constabulary (RUC) and his wife, at Hillsborough Castle. Newman was promoted to Chief Constable in May 1976 and was knighted for his work with the RUC about the same time as this photograph was taken, in 1978. His tenure continued into the early Thatcher years, until 1980. Mason got on well with Newman whom he regarded as 'strict in his observation of the law and as straight as a die'. One area in which they had some success was in creating a better relationship between the Army and the RUC. (MA)

Detail from a Jak (Raymond Jackson, 1927-97) cartoon. Mason, pipe in mouth, is portrayed marching into an ancient Irish Maze (prison), with Merlyn Reece and Jim Callaghan exchanging comments. As Northern Ireland Secretary of State, Reece had put an end to Special Category status as from 1 March 1976, six months before Mason's arrival in the Province. After that date those convicted of scheduled terrorist offences were housed in eight new 'H-blocks' at the former RAF station at Long Kesh which became officially known as HM Prison Maze. (MCA/Raymond Jackson)

After transfer to the H-blocks inmates began to refuse to wear their prison uniforms, wrapping themselves in bed sheets in 'blanket protest', reinforcing their claim that they were not criminals but political prisoners. By 1978 300 men were involved but guards refused to allow the prisoners to use the toilets without wearing proper uniform. In turn this and other restrictions led to the 'dirty protest', inmates defecating in their cells and smearing excrement on the walls, a situation which continued when the Thatcher government began in 1979. This postcard, dated 20 April 1979, was sent to Mason, from Jeu Vaessen of the Dutch 'Vitg. Ierland Komitee' , with a simple message on the reverse: TREAT PEOPLE HUMAN. (MA)

Mason wants Ulster news black-outs

Headline from the *Observer* newspaper, 23 January 1977. Earlier in the month Mason had met the governors of the BBC and other prominent Ulster figures for a private dinner at the Culloden Hotel, Belfast. Asked to say a few words, he expressed his dismay in frank terms concerning the 'cheapjack journalism', comparing the BBC's coverage to that of the *Sun* and *Daily Mirror*. He was particularly annoyed that the BBC broadcast a critical profile about him in their *Spotlight* programme, after he had refused to take part. Editors were not happy when the news leaked, the *Observer* also citing a letter that he had written to members of major public bodies asking them not to divulge security sensitive information to the Press. Mason was unrepentant, later saying that though he was not in favour of censorship he believed that 'journalists have a duty to be especially careful when reporting a terrorist campaign which seeks to overthrow a civil society'. (The Observer)

Mason on a typical walkabout in Belfast. Although obviously well protected, he wanted to try and portray as much normality as possible. (MA)

An informal chat with the troops but note the careful police and Army protection. (MA)

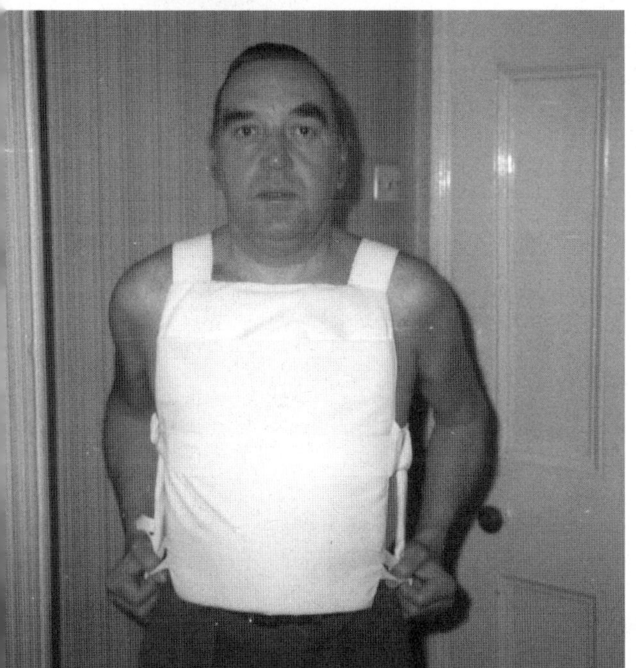

Demonstrating the kind of body armour vest worn under garments, this one dating from April 1979. (MA)

A more discrete form of vest was worn on many later occasions, this example produced by the Second Chance company and on display at Cawthorne Victorian Museum, near Barnsley. (BEC)

A group of Belfast boys from St Patrick's Secondary School, Antrim Road, Belfast, have tea with Mason in his Westminster office after a visit to the House of Commons in their half-term holiday, 24 February 1977. Also present, second left of Mason, is Gerry Fitt, the Belfast Dock MP and Leader of the Social Democratic and Labour Party. Just over two years later, Fitt, unhappy about government policy in Northern Ireland, abstained from the crucial Commons vote which led to Labour's defeat in the May general election. (MA)

With the popular DJ, radio and television personality Jimmy Savile, 29 September 1977. Mason was always keen to improve the Northern Ireland economy and took opportunity to publicise developments whenever he could. This occasion, in his London office, concerned the promotion of the Londonderry-built Viking bicycles. Famous for *Top of The Pops* appearances and *Jim I'll Fix It,* Saville was also a keen cyclist and long-distance runner. The two Yorkshiremen had other interests too, Saville having had experience as a young miner, recruited as a Bevin Boy. (MA)

On 10 October 1977 Mason flew to Washington for a ten-day industrial promotion tour in order to encourage American industry to invest in Ulster. At Heathrow he had a chance meeting with an old friend, Field-Marshal Lord Carver who was then Commissioner-Designate for Rhodesia. Carver was there to meet the UN's Special representative for Rhodesia, Lieut-Gen Prem Chand of India but the latter's plane was delayed. (MA)

Strike or I will quit, says Paisley

The proposed Loyalist strike, in part led by the Reverend Ian Paisley, Member of Parliament for North Antrim and leader of the the Democratic Unionist Party (DUP) which he co-founded in 1971 was regarded by Mason 'as the most dangerous threat to Northern Ireland' during his tenure as Secretary of State. The strike, scheduled for 3 May 1977, never matched the one organised in 1974. Paisley's threat (on 30 April) to resign if the Loyalists' call was unanswered did not take place either. Paisley's return to a barricaded Ballymena led to Mason singing *Don't Cry for Me, Ballymena* as he took off by helicopter from Stormont Castle, on 10 May. The headline is taken from the *Observer* newspaper of 1 May 1977, the prelude to John Cole's report in which he reports that Mason had agreed to meet Paisley and the other main player, Ernest Baird, leader of the short-lived United Ulster Unionists Party (UUUP). (MA)

Welcome jobs boost for Belfast

Typical headline (6 August 1978) following Mason's announcement that the De Lorean Motor Company were to build a new car factory near Belfast which would result in a rapid build-up of 2,000 jobs, with the promise of 3,400 within six years. The most extraordinary and ultimately the most disastrous attempt to boost the Northern Ireland and particularly the Belfast economy concerned successive governments' investments in the ill-fated Company. De Lorean had developed a futuristic stainless steel bodied and gull-winged sports car, targeted at the US market. 'It will be a great boost for Ulster,' said Mason, and a 'hammer blow' to the IRA. Substantial incentives were offered for a new factory to be built on a greenfield site at Dunmurry, West Belfast. When Mason got cabinet approval, on 3 August 1978, he believed that he had 'won a glittering prize'. (The Observer)

The flamboyant American John Zachary Delorean (1925-2005) and the prototype of the DMC-12 sports car. By April 1981 £84 million of public money had been handed over to the Company, about £30 million coming from Margaret Thatcher's so-called anti-subsidy government. The factory started manufacturing in 1981 (producing over 9,000 cars) but went into receivership and closed amid recriminations and bitterness in November 1982, following DeLorean's arrest on drug trafficking charges (for which he was found not guilty). It was not until 1998, following a court decision in favour of the UK government against the Arthur Anderson accountancy firm (subsequently found guilty for its role in the 2002 Enron scandal) that any compensation was received. A DeLorean was immortalised as the time machine in the *Back to the Future* film trilogy. (DMC)

Provos rounded up after blast

from a Staff Reporter in Belfast

MURDER MURDER
MURDER MURDER MURDER MURDER
This is what the bombers did

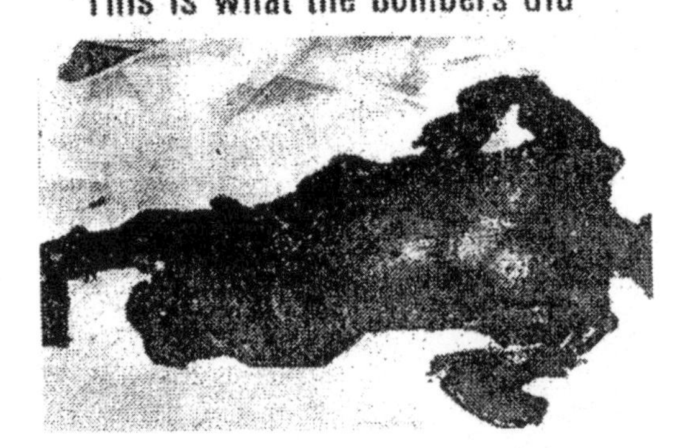

Typical newspaper headline of 19 August 1978 following the La Mon House hotel restaurant bombing at Comber, near Belfast, two days earlier, which resulted in 12 deaths and 30 people seriously injured. The innocent victims were attending a dinner held by the Irish Collie Club. It was described by Mason as 'one of the worst acts of terrorist savagery since the Troubles began'. The grim leaflet to the right of the headline was produced by the RUC with Mason's authority. The 'Provos rounded up' consisted of 20 suspected IRA members including a young Gerry Adams but none were ever convicted. The Observer

Marjorie Mason (fifth from the right) and a group of Army wives at Stormont in April 1978. Marjorie commuted between Barnsley, London and Belfast fortnightly and played an active role in meeting Army and Royal Ulster Constabulary wives. She was also keen to participate in local, non-political events, attending and speaking at coffee mornings, school prize-givings, as well as visiting hospitals and factories. (MA)

Taking time off, fishing at Strangford Lough, County Down, in 1978. It was a momentous day. Mason with a prize catch from Strangford Lough: a 50lb tope. It was a good job his security team were on hand to help land the specimen. (MA)

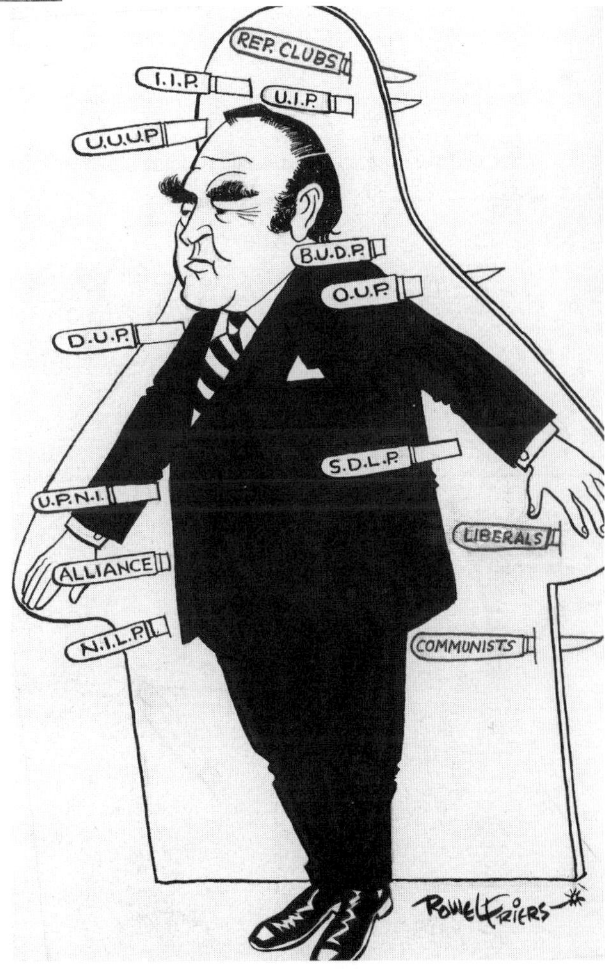

This original artwork was presented to Mason by the most well known cartoonists of the Troubles, Rowel Friers (1920-98) and sums up better than many words the kind of pressure that was placed on the Secretary of State for Northern Ireland. Friers, honoured by an MBE in 1977, produced work for the *Belfast News*, *Belfast Telegraph*, *Irish Times* as well as several English newspapers. (MCA/Rowel Friers)

Meeting Irish sports stars and personalities at a fund raising reception in London:
(1) Danny Blanchflower (centre), the former Barnsley, Aston Villa, Tottenham Hotspur and Northern Ireland footballer, and golfer Fred Daly who won the Open at Royal Liverpool in 1947, the first (and only, until 2007) Irishman to achieve this feat. (MA)
(2) Enjoying the occasion with Northern Ireland athlete Mary Peters MBE who had won a gold medal for the pentathlon in the 1972 Olympics held in Munich. (MA)

With HM the Queen and Duke of Edinburgh at a tree planting ceremony at Hillsborough Castle, part of the Silver Jubilee visit to Northern Ireland, Wednesday 10 August 1977. On the same day the Masons dined with the Queen on board the Royal Yacht *Britannia*, staying the night on board. The next day's royal visit to the new University of Ulster's Coleraine campus was a very nervous one since Mason had been warned of a genuine bomb threat, with little time to change all the planning. Fortunately no harm was done, the Queen, Prince Philip and Prince Andrew meeting the people; but in the evening after they had left, a small bomb did explode in the university grounds. (MA)

A rare photograph taken inside the Cabinet Room of 10 Downing Street in 1978. Mason, with his ever-present pipe, sits next to Tony Benn and across from Roy Hattersley. Prime Minister James Callaghan enjoys a joke with the cameraman. The Leader of the Commons, Michael Foot, sits to Callaghan's left. (MA)

Seated on the Front Bench between Prime Minister James Callaghan and Home Secretary Merlyn Reece, awaiting the summons to hear the Queen's Speech, November 1977. (MA)

At home, in Barnsley, walking with Oscar, the Masons' dalmation dog, c. 1978. To Mason's immediate left is the tall figure of his parliamentary agent Trevor Lindley, and next to him a long standing friend and Barnsley Councillor, Ron Fisher. Journalist Ron Kershaw is on the right and a ubiquitous protection officer is in the background. (Roy Sabine)

Passing-out parade photograph at the Royal Ulster Constabulary Training centre, Enniskillen, 4 April 1979. Mason is near the centre of the seated row, between (left) Superintendent A McCaffrey (Commandant) and (right) Sir Kenneth Newman (Chief Constable). Founded in 1922, the RUC changed its name to the Police Service of Northern Ireland (PSNI) in 2001. (MA)

Part Eight

Under Threat

Shadow Minister and Backbencher 1979-87

'I would always have the satisfaction of knowing that I never gave anything less than my best. If an MP can honestly say that at the end of his Commons career, he hasn't done too badly.'

Marjorie and Roy Mason cast their vote in Barnsley at the General Election, 3 May 1979. (MA)

Life and Times

1979 [3/4.5] General Election: the Tories win and have an overall majority of 43; and now the nation has its first woman Prime Minister, 53-year-old Margaret Thatcher. In Barnsley, Roy Mason retains his Barnsley seat, attracting 36,276 votes, a Labour majority of 22,622.

[4] Callaghan appoints Mason as Shadow Spokesperson on Agriculture, Fisheries and Food.

[5] A 'hit team' was sent from Ulster to kill Mason but was put off by the level of security in Barnsley.

[27.8] Lord Mountbatten is assassinated by IRA at Mullaghmore, County Sligo.
Warrenpoint, South Down: 18 British soldiers killed by an IRA bombing ambush.

[8] Struggle between Left and Right in Barnsley consistency party begins in earnest. Mason criticised by the Left.

[2.10] Labour Party Conference votes for mandatory re-selection of Labour MPs.

[8.10] In an unprecedented speech for a former Secretary of State for Northern Ireland, Mason describes what it is like to live under a constant threat of assassination.

[21.12] Marriage of Jill Mason (Roy and Marjorie's youngest daughter) to Kevin Martin.

1980 [2.1] National steel strike begins.

[28.2] Barnsley constituency AGM, Mason's political future now under question as Left takes more control.

[1.4] Steel strike ends.

[18.4] Robert Mugabe is Prime Minister of an independent Zimbabwe.

[22.4] Unemployment over 1.5 million.

[1.5] American businessman Ian MacGregor is new head of British Steel Corporation.

[5.5] SAS storm Iranian Embassy in London, freeing hostages.

[8.6] Wave of bombings in Ulster.

[17.6] Francis Pym, Secretary of State for Defence, announces that US Cruise missiles will be located at two RAF bases: Greenham Common and Molesworth.

[31.7] Shirley Williams, William Rodgers and David Owen urge Labour MPs to join them against the far left.

[27.8] UK unemployment reaches 2 million.

[21.9] CND rally at Greenham Common.

[10] Labour Party Conference endorses reselection of MPs.

[10.10] Margaret Thatcher's 'the lady is not for turning' speech at the Conservative Party Conference.

[27.10] Yorkshire Miners' Council, chaired by Arthur Scargill, passes motion calling on all mining MPs to vote for Michael Foot in forthcoming leadership election.

[31.10] Barnsley General Management Committe (Labour Party) also recommends voting for Foot in leadership election.
Mason defies 'threats' and refuses to say who he will support in the Labour leadership election.

[20.11] Boundary Commission proposes split of Barnsley constituency into Central and East (based on the town) and West (replacing Penistone but also including Worsbrough). Mason would be on 'safer' ground in Barnsley Central.

[4.11] Mason ignores YMC and BGC and votes for Denis Healey.
Michael Foot is elected leader of the Labour Party. Foot asks Mason to continue as Shadow Agriculture minister.

1981 [1] Labour Party special conference at Wembley 'widens the franchise' for future leadership elections.

[25.1] The 'Gang of Four': William Rodgers, Roy Jenkins, Shirley Williams and David Owen form a Council for Social Democracy. Mason refuses to join them.

[2] Mason forms the Triple Alliance, involving the Unions and sponsored MPs.

[10.2] The National Coal Board (NCB) announce a major pit closure programme affecting thousands of miners' jobs and NUM threaten a national strike.

[12.2] Ian Paisley suspended from the House of Commons for using 'unparliamentary language' against the Secretary of State for Northern Ireland.

[18.2] Thatcher government withdraws plans to close 23 pits after meeting with Joe Gormley and the NUM.

[14.3] Mason wins reselection vote in Barnsley by 61 votes to 53.

[26.3] Social Democratic Party (SDP) launched.

[5.5] Maze hunger striker Bobby Sands dies after a 66-day fast.

[30.5] People's March for Jobs reaches London.

[10.6] Eight IRA prisoners escape from Crumlin Road prison.

[16.6] Liberal Party and SDP form an alliance.

[29.7] Royal Wedding: Prince Charles and Lady Diana Spencer.

[8] Energy Secretary Nigel Lawson regards Mason as 'the ideal choice' to replace Derek Ezra as Chairman of the NCB.

[27.9] Denis Healey narrowly wins election to be deputy leader (under new electoral system) under a challenge from Tony Benn.
Mason supports Healey again.

[10] NUM President Joe Gormley recommends Mason to Nigel Lawson as successor to Ezra at the Coal Board.

[3.10] Hunger strike in Maze prison ends after ten deaths.

[10.10] Chelsea Barracks bombed by IRA and 2 killed.

	[24.10]	CND march in London attracts 250,000 people.
	[11]	Michael Foot attends Remembrance Sunday ceremony wearing a 'duffle coat', causing offence.
	[8.12]	Arthur Scargill elected President of the NUM.
1982	[26.1]	Unemployment passes 3 million for first time since 1930s.
	[19.2]	De Lorean Motor Car Company goes into receivership in Belfast. Argentines land on South Georgia Island.
	[22.3]	Mason reselected in Barnsley by 61 votes to 53.
	[2.4]	Start of Falklands War.
	[14.6]	Fighting ends in the Falklands.
	[6/7]	Barnsley GMC demand British withdrawal from the War. Mason organises a civic reception for Falklands service people.
	[2.7]	Roy Jenkins is elected leader of the new SDP.
	[20.7]	Hyde Park and Regents Park IRA bombs kills 8 soldiers, with 47 people wounded.
	[4.10]	Presentation of scrolls (idea of Mason) to Falklands veterans at Barnsley.
	[11.10]	Wreck of *Mary Rose*, flagship of Henry VIII raised.
	[19.10]	De Lorean factory in Belfast closes with the loss of 1,500 jobs.
	[21.10]	Sinn Fein win first seats in Northern Ireland Assembly and Gerry Adams is elected MP for Belfast West.
	[6.12]	Ballykelly bomb kills 16 people and injures 66.
1983	[22.2]	In Parliament Mason strongly opposes possible appointment of Ian MacGregor to the Coal Board.
	[28.2]	Yorkshire and South Wales miners strike over planned pit closures.
	[2.]	Mason now a back-bench MP.
	[28.3]	Energy Secretary Nigel Lawson announces that British Steel Corporation chairman Ian MacGregor will be the new chairman of the NCB (as from 1 September).
	[9.6]	General Election: Conservatives win with a landslide majority. Divided Labour Party under Michael Foot only get 28% of the vote. Mason's majority down to 14,000.
	[14.6]	David Owen is new leader of the SDP (replacing Roy Jenkins).
	[12.6]	Michael Foot resigns as Labour leader.
	[13.6]	Roy Jenkins resigns as SDP leader.
	[3.7]	Gerry Fitt's home destroyed by fire.
	[7.]	Mason opposes restoration of hanging for terrorists.
	[23.9]	Thirty-eight IRA prisoners escape from the Maze prison.
	[2.10]	Mason votes for Hattersley in Labour Party leadership election. Neil Kinnock wins, Hattersley becomes Deputy Leader.
	[22.10]	Huge anti-nuclear demonstration in London organised by CND attracts over one million supporters.

[17.12] Bomb explosion outside Harrods kills six and injures many.

1984 [15.1] Tony Benn re-enters Parliament as MP for Chesterfield following his defeat in Bristol West at the last General Election.
[26.1] Governor of Maze prison resigns following critical report on recent escapes.
[1.3] NCB announces plans of a major cut in coal production equal to the closure of 20 pits or 20,000 jobs, including Cortonwood Colliery.
[5.3] Many Yorkshire miners on strike.
[6.3] Scottish and Yorkshire areas of NUM call for official strike action. NUM Executive calls all members to strike.
[12.3] National miners' strike against proposed pit closures starts.
[14.3] Attempted assassination of West Belfast MP Gerry Adams.
[15.3] Young Yorkshire miner David Jones killed whilst on picket duty at Ollerton, Nottinghamshire.
[9.4] Over 100 striking miners arrested at Cresswell Colliery, Nottinghamshire.
[12.4] NUM Executive rules out a national union ballot to continue the strike.
[14.5] Mass rally of miners in Mansfield, Nottinghamshire.
[4.5] Large demonstration of miners at Harworth, Nottinghamshire.
[29.5] Mass pickets and police clash at Orgreave, near Rotherham.
[30.5] Arthur Scargill arrested for obstruction at Orgreave.
[15.6] Yorkshire miner Joe Green killed whilst picketing at Ferrybridge.
[18.6] Thousands of miners and police clash at 'Battle of Orgreave'. Many injured, including Arthur Scargill.
[21.9] Mass pickets clash with police at Maltby Colliery.
[22.9] The Bishop of Durham refers to the Coal Board Chairman Ian MacGregor as an 'imported, elderly American'.
[28.9] Justice Nichols rules that the miners' strike is 'illegal'.
[12.10] IRA bomb kills four people and injures many at the Grand Hotel, Brighton, during the Conservative Party Conference.
[25.10] Court orders seizure of NUM assets after failure to pay a £200,000 fine.
[31.10] ACAS talks between NCB and NUM break down.
[30.11] Two miners charged with murdering taxi driver David Wilkie by dropping a concrete block on his car from a motorway bridge.

1985 [27.2] NCB claim that over half of its workforce have returned to work.
[28.2] Nine police killed in IRA bomb attack on Newry police station.
[3.3] NUM delegate conference votes to end year-long miners' strike as from 5 March.
[5] Barnsley Central consituency: Mason easily wins reselection, by 59 votes to 19.
[5] Mason leads all-party delegation to Moscow.

[13.7] Live Aid concerts.
[19.10] Union of Democratic Mineworkers (UDM) established by miners from Nottinghamshire and Derbyshire.
[15.11] Anglo-Irish Agreement signed at Hillsborough Castle.

1986 [9.1] Michael Heseltine resigns from Thatcher's Cabinet.
[20] Anglo-French agreement on a twin tunnel Channel rail link.
[26.4] Chernobyl nuclear reactor disaster in Soviet Union.
[10.6] Patrick Magee found guilty of Brighton Grand Hotel bombing.
[12.6] Derek Hatton, leader of Liverpool council expelled from Labour Party for his Militant Tendency associations.
[24.6] Ian Paisley's DUP protest against the dissolution of the Northern Ireland Assembly.
[23.10] Mason informs Barnsley Labour Party and issues a press statement to say that he will be retiring as an MP at the next General Election.

1987 [20.1] Terry Waite, Archbishop of Canterbury's special envoy, is abducted in Beirut.
[25.4] Car bomb kills Lord Justice Gibson and Lady Gibson in Ireland.
[8.5] Nine IRA gunmen killed in a battle with police and soldiers in County Armagh.
[11.6] General Election: Conservatives returned with a majority of 01 and Margaret Thatcher begins her third consecutive term of office.
[11.6] Roy Mason raised to Peerage.

Overview

This part of the book covers Mason's final years as an MP, from the aftermath of Labour's election defeat in June 1979 to his retirement from the Commons before the 1987 General Election. With James Callaghan still leader, he was offered and accepted the position of Shadow Minister for Agriculture, Fisheries and Food. Mason continued in this role during much of the Michael Foot era but then returned to the back benches, after more than two decades of occupying posts of responsibility.

Earlier, the parlous state of the minority Callaghan administration was intensified during the 1978/79 Winter of Discontent and an election was perhaps expected sooner rather than later in the New Year. The Government had become reliant on support via arrangements with smaller parties, and especially with the Liberals. A vote of no confidence tabled by the Conservatives on the night of 28 March resulted in a humiliating defeat by just one vote (311-310) for Labour, forcing Callaghan to call a general election, the first time that this had happened to any Prime Minister since Ramsey McDonald in 1924. Labour fingers pointed in the direction of Gerry Fitt whose support would have saved the government. Many years later, in the BBC documentary *The Night the Government Fell* (2004) Fitt blamed his decision to abstain (though denying 'personal conflict' initially) on a dislike of Mason, not wanting him to continue as Secretary of State for Northern Ireland. In fairness, Fitt also despised Callaghan's tactics to get him on board. A curious non-voter was a former pub landlord, the Irish Nationalist MP Frank Maguire, who made a rare Commons appearance, ostensibly to make his maiden speech and vote, subsequently referred to by Shirley Williams as the 'lost leprechaun'.

Mason admits that he did not expect Labour to win the 1979 election, comparing the Left to the Bevanites of the fifties and referring to the recent power of the unions as damaging the 'weakest and vulnerable' in society. In Barnsley, there was a small (1.9%) swing against Labour but he won with a 22,622 majority, and against two more candidates than in 1974. One of these was Brendan Gallagher, representing a Troops Out of Ireland group. Gallagher's involvement attracted considerable post-election controversy (even though he only attracted 638 votes), due to his nomination paper being signed by two local Labour men.

The relatively peripheral Shadow Agriculture post was not one that Mason would have preferred, even after enduring an exhausting three years in Northern Ireland. But even a casual glance through Hansard and the national press shows that he was a more than active spokesperson. Amongst his early campaigns included speeches against the unrestricted import of continental milk into Britain (1979); on France's refusal to comply with a European Court order to trade freely in sheep meat (1980); the sale of surplus Common Market to the Soviet Union (which he felt would benefit 'aggressive' Afghanistan, 1980); for a ban on the pesticide 245T because it could harm farm workers (1980); against Peter Walker's (the Minister of Agriculture) decision to end EEC compensation to British farmers (which would increase food prices, 1980); and also criticising Walker 'reneging' on his commitment to reach a fair deal for UK's fishing rights in Common Market waters (1980).

But undoubtedly the greatest threat to Mason in the first few years of Opposition concerned the growing Left and Right struggle within his own consituency party, especially after the October conference when mandatory reselection of MPs was agreed. Certainly in the press, national and local, the rift was far too personalised, often as Scargill versus Mason or Scargallites against the Right. As early as August 1979 a motion from the Monk Bretton branch called on the consituency to dissociate itself 'from the political attitude of its MP' (amended to 'any MP' after a proposal by Arthur Scargill and approved by the General Management Committee) and was subsequently warned that he would have to undergo 'the biggest conversion since Saul' (County Councillor Jack Brown, quoted in the Guardian, 15.12.79) if he is to remain as MP. Mason refused to be drawn into the melee, only saying that it would be far better if every member of the constituency party was consulted by ballot about a candidate.

Mason faced further pressure during 1980 after the Left increased their influence in the GMC. He countered by saying that the criticism was just what Roy Jenkins and others needed to attract disaffected members to support their growing campaign for a new Centre party. Within just three months the Barnsley Conservative Association increased its membership from 60 to 1200, according to its chairman, Paul Sykes, reported by Michael Parkin in the Guardian (8.9.80). Subsequently, Mason refused to have anything to do with what soon became the Social Democratic Party (SDP).

Matters came to a head in late October 1980 when the Barnsley GMC voted overwhelmingly (31st, 92-22) in favour of backing Michael Foot in the Labour leadership election, demanding that their MP should support him, a decision similar to that which had been taken a few days earlier (27th) by the Yorkshire Miners' Council, who also ruled that any mining MP who did not vote for Foot would not get the support of the Union 'in any future reselection process'. Mason would not budge, saying he would not yield to threats and would 'use his own judgement' about his vote. Mason's parliamentary agent, Trevor Lindley, bemoaned that the party of Gaitskell 'no longer exists', placing the local blame on the 'Left-wing block vote controlled by Mr Arthur Scargill', according to a feature article by Max Hastings in the *New Standard* (22.1.81). Hastings was convinced that in the forthcoming reselection process, set within the existing consituency boundaries, 'nothing can save him [Mason]'.

Mason voted for Healey in the Labour leadership election, Michael Foot winning by only 10 votes. Mason did not see Foot, in his late sixties, as the kind of modern leader to command wide appeal among Labour voters and thought that he would have 'minimum' impact in the country as a whole.

Throughout difficult months before his own reselection Mason remained consistent in condemning 'Labour rebels' who had left or considered leaving the party, attracted by an 'electoral alliance in the centre of British politics'. He also warned of the potential 'disaffection' among 'a substantial number of Labour MPs' if an electoral college was endorsed at the special conference held at Wembley on 24 January 1981.

But Mason did survive the weekend reselection vote in Barnsley (13.3.82), albeit by a narrow margin (61-53) over arch critic Jack Brown. Much of his support came from party ward nominations and trade unions, and he still managed eight votes from the NUM.

Earlier, in the summer and autumn of 1981, word was going around Westminster that Mason was favourite to take over as Chairman of the NCB. Energy Secretary Nigel Lawson in his autobiography certainly confirms his own interest (via Keith Joseph) in Mason for the job, and also that of the then NUM President Joe Gormley (Lawson, 156). In the event of course it was 70-year-old Ian MacGregor, that 'geriatic American butcher' (Scargill, quoted in MacGregor, 64/65) who Margaret Thatcher appointed to antagonise the miners (and a good number of Tories too) throughout the 1984/85 strike which Mason regarded as 'the greatest tragedy ever to have overcome the coal industry'. Despite the well known animosity between Mason and Scargill one wonders if aspects of the strike would have been so bitter if Thatcher had acted on Lawson's early advice. In remuneration alone MaGregor's appointment was costly, £1.5 million having to be paid to Lazard Freres of New York (where MacGregor was a partner) in compensation.

There is no doubt that the so-called Falkland's factor revived a flagging Tory administration during 1982 and provided a desperately needed boost for Margaret Thatcher whose popularity in the country had fallen to an all-time low for any prime minister within living memory. De-industrialisation and monetarism were not welcome in South Yorkshire. In Barnsley, as the Task Force sailed towards the South Atlantic, the GMC had passed a resolution calling for the British to withdraw from the war. A dismayed Mason disagreed with the decision which he said was against national party policy anyway. The former Defence Secretary, whose campaign to keep the Harrier jet was to prove a decisive component in the defeat of the Argentine forces, countered the GMC's by contacting the Mayor, Councillor Ken Rispin, himself a former D-Day veteran. The resultant proposal for a civic reception in honour of Barnsley's Falkland service people was accepted by the Council. Mason's suggestion for the presentation of a memorial scroll also came to fruition. The event, which attracted widespread publicity, involving some 82 veterans and their families, took place in Barnsley Civic Hall on Monday 4 October 1982, Grimethorpe Colliery Band providing an appropriate musical background. The most moving part of the ceremony occurred when Jack Atkinson from Grimethorpe received the scroll from Mayor Rispin on behalf of his son, Warrant Officer Malcolm Atkinson, who was killed when a Sea King helicopter in which he was a passenger crashed. Mason concluded his speech on the day by saying 'Thanks to you our local sons - Barnsley salutes you today.'

By the time of the expected early election which was announced for 9 June 1983 Mason was a backbench MP and far from happy about Labour's 'half-baked' Manifesto, famously described by Gerald Kaufman as 'the longest suicide note in history'. Labour was almost beaten into third place in the total number of votes cast, the Conservatives triumphing with a majority of 144 seats, and a momentum which kept them in power until 1997. Mason fought his last election with his usual style 'knocking on doors [and] bellowing through a loudspeaker' but could 'sense the unhappiness' compared with previous campaigns. His majority was down to just over 14,000, the Conservative (Howard Oldfield) and Lib/Alliance (Rev Geoffrey Reid) candidates sharing about the same number of votes cast for Mason between them.

Throughout the year long miners' strike Mason was critical of the Thatcher government's handling of the dispute, and the 'ruthless determination' of the Prime Minister to 'win at all costs'. On 7 June 1984, for example, he asked the Leader of the House (John Biffen) to 'explain why the Prime Minister constantly misled the House about her involvement in the miners' dispute...' (Hansard, V.61/442) and got little response other than that the PM and Government 'have paid proper and prudent regard to the national interest'. On the 14th of the same month Mason questioned the coal stock figures of Energy Secretary (Peter Walker) as well as his refusal to intervene in the dispute' (*Hansard*, V.61/622). Then on the 19th he questioned the Secretary of State for Employment (Alan Clark) about the number of redundant mineworkers 'denied unemployment benefits' even where they were given notice before the strike commenced. Towards the end of the month, on 28 June, during PM's Question Time, he asked Margaret Thatcher to 'become a promotor of conciliation between the National Coal Board and the National Union of Mineworkers, instead of standing by and allowing the coal industry to fall into disrepair and gradual destruction' (*Hansard*, V.62/1154). Mrs Thatcher's reply included reference to 'an excellent pay settlement' being available and all mining unions sitting down to discuss the Plan for Coal. Towards the end of the strike he spoke during the Coal Industry Debate, saying that it 'is a Government-inspired, political strike' (Hansard, V.72/626) and continued to press for police records of arrested miners who were not charged to be erased and the granting of an amnesty for all those acquitted (eg 4

March 1985, *Hansard*,V.74/660).

But Mason was equally unhappy about the way the NUM and in particular Arthur Scargill 'had been aching for confrontation ever since he became national President'. He considered the 6 March decision of the Union's Executive to call out all the coalfields on strike 'crazily irresponsible' (Mason, 243), since it was 'a fact of life' that some pits have to close due to exhaustion of reserves and geological problems, so had to close on economic grounds. It was 'the only way to maintain a thriving industry and preserve long-term jobs'. Scargill did not want a single job to be lost. Mason was on sound ground when he questioned the NUM's tactics, striking at the end of winter, when the demand for coal was beginning to fall. In fact the NCB via Nigel Lawson and the Government had been preparing stock piles at power stations for two years. Mason believed that the Union's greatest mistake, however, was not calling for a national ballot which predictably lost much of the support of the Nottinghamshire miners and 'allowed the Tories to claim the moral high ground'.

In the depth of winter conditions were miserable in the mining communities of the Barnsley area, as they were in other coalfield communities. The Masons did what they could to help strikers' families and children. From the back bench and through parliamentary questions he continued to campaign for justice regarding the many ordinary miners who had been unfairly arrested, fingerprinted or denied unemployment benefit.

The new Labour leader Neil Kinnock, like Mason, from a deeply rooted mining family and constituency, found the strike a disturbing experience and - at least privately - also believed the strike to be doomed without a ballot of rank and file miners. He publicly criticised picket line violence and mass picketing which he knew alienated public opinion. For both men the tragedy was that it was a strike by the very men who had contributed so much to the making of the Labour Party; and their antipathy to Arthur Scargill was equally vehement. It was perhaps Kinnock, however, rather than back bencher Mason who was to be damaged the most, his leadership affected as was Labour's electoral recovery.

On safer ground in Barnsley Central after the boundary changes, Mason easily won the next reselection meeting, in May 1985, by 59 votes to 18, against Adult Training Centre manager, Joe Power who was secretary of the constituency party.

One of Mason's last official overseas visits, leading an all-party delegation to Russia, resulted in him campaigning and speaking in the House on 13 November 1986 about the plight of 'refuseniks', Jewish people who were not allowed by the Soviet Union to return to their families in Israel and elsewhere. The publicity that he engendered about this freedom issue was much appreciated by the Board of Deputies of British Jews who thanked him for his 'superb speech' in the adjournment debate.

Another threat to Mason during his final years as an MP was far more serious than reselection. It was the threat on his life. After the Neave and Mountbatten assassinations his personal security was extremely high but living with this is hard to comprehend. Jim Callaghan, speaking to Tony Benn on 12 September 1979, was certainly concerned: 'Poor old Roy Mason is deeply worried; he has absolutely maximum security but still he's afraid of what they'll do to him (Benn, 534).'

A short time later, on 8 October, Mason spoke in unprecedented detail at a private luncheon in Barnsley about the pressures placed on his family. His comments, to the Newspaper Society, received national press coverage (eg *The Guardian*, 9.10.79). He said that he was now 'living the life of a recluse' but had decided 'to speak out about personal problems associated with the job...so that anyone in public life who received a death threat from the IRA should take it very seriously'. Mason also eerily described the new 'competition to kill' between the IRA and INLA, so the press and public 'should be aware of it'. He told listeners that he was 'not frightened' by the threats since his home in Barnsley had become 'a miniature fortress'. The gardens were patrolled, floodlights were on throughout the night, and armed security officers lived outside on a 24-hour rota. Visitors were checked, even the postman and milkman. When out walking his dog or shopping he was surrounded by armed security men. Mrs Mason, when asked about the pressure, stoically replied 'I am still living with him, aren't I?' Mason told the audience that he had been informed that hit squads had travelled to Barnsley during the recent general election, intending to kill him. Finally, he said that he would be 'forever grateful' for the police protection and the major security exercise which had put off the assassins. 'Forever' was the right word.

After speaking to Neil Kinnock (who was to recommend him for a Life peerage), Mason wrote to his Barnsley Labour Party colleagues on 23 October 1986, informing them of his intention to retire at the next general election, when he would be 63. His letter concluded on an upbeat note: 'I am leaving at time when the Labour Party is on the move led by a realistic and revivalist Leader who has quite remarkably restored the Party from the debacle of 1983 to a belief in victory in 1987. No better time to announce I am standing down.'

Mason (centre) outside the Barnsley Labour Party Committee Rooms during the General Election campaign. To his immediate left is his agent, Trevor Lindley and Councillor Eric Denton. Standing on the right is Councillor Theo Hinchcliffe. (MA)

Caricatures of politicians grace the covers of *The House Magazine*, the weekly journal of the Houses of Parliament. This original drawing of Roy Mason appeared on the May 21-27 1979 edition (No 97, vol 5). It was the work of a regular contributor, the Welsh cartoonist Glan Williams (1911-86) who presented the original to Mason for the latter's growing cartoon archive. Inside, under the heading 'Roy Steps Out', the editorial refers to his 'return to the Opposition benches from the rigours of the Northern Ireland Office. (MCA/Glan Williams)

Just like old times. In 'pit muck', caught by a Barnsley photographer just as he had surfaced from an underground visit to a local colliery protection officers 'in tow'. To Mason's right is a parliamentary colleague, Allen McKay, who had been elected as MP for the Penistone constituency in 1978. His seat was abolished in the boundary changes when it was contested as Barnsley West in 1983, McKay continuing to serve until he retired at the 1992 Election. This photograph dates from about 1980. (Roy Sabine)

Mason told to 'see the light'

Mason hits back

Labour Left ousts Mason's backers

Mr Mason and the big drop

Left presses Mason

THE BATTLE FOR THE LABOUR PARTY: Scargill takes off gloves in fight with MP

Mason defies Scargill

It's the Barnsley chop ...

Typical headlines in newspapers during the 1979/80 period when Mason came under increasing threat of reselection. (Guardian/Barnsley Star/Sheffield Morning Telegraph/ Sheffield Star)

At home, enjoying a Christmas drink with his great friend, the famous cricket umpire Harold 'Dickie' Bird, 1981. (MA)

As Shadow Minister for Agriculture, Food and Fisheries, and subsequently as a backbencher, Mason was involved in a variety of events at home and abroad, on this occasion (12 February 1981) attending a dinner at 10 Downing Street in honour of the Prime Minister of of Mauritius, Sir Seewoosangor Ramgoolan and Lady Ramgoolam. The island of Mauritius, located about 550 miles from Madagascar, off east coast of the African continent, had gained its independence under Sir Ramgoolan in 1968. (MA)

Major Malcolm MacLeod of the Royal Marines signs the Visitors' Book in Barnsley Town Hall during the civic reception to Falklands War veterans, 4 October 1982. Wing Commander I E Francis, Acting Station Master at RAF Finningley looks on, along with the Mayor of Barnsley, Councillor Kenneth Rispin, the Mayoress, Shelagh Haywood, Roy Mason MP (whose idea for the occasion it was) and Dearne Valley MP Edwin Wainwright. (MA)

Barnsley Metropolitan Borough Council

4th October, 1982

Victory in the Falklands

"In commemoration of the extraordinary feat of arms of the Armed Forces of the Crown and their civilian colleagues who, following the illegal invasion of the Falkland Islands by Argentine Forces on 2nd April 1982, sailed from the United Kingdom in a powerful task force, and following fierce fighting, obtained the surrender of the Argentine Forces on 14th June 1982.

This scroll is in proud recognition of the part played in that operation by . . . .

Those taking part in the successful campaign to repossess the Islands showed the bravery, the courage, the skill and the dedication which is in the finest traditions of the Armed Forces and which has served our nation so well over so many centuries. The people of this country, of the Falkland Islands and of all other countries who value the rights of peoples to live in freedom, will never forget their heroism, nor the sacrifice of those who failed to return.

What stands if freedom falls?"

Charles Kenneth Rispin   Mayor of Barnsley

Copy of the certificate, inscribed on vellum, presented to 82 Falklands veterans at a special ceremony held in Barnsley Civic Hall. The most moving moment was when Jack Atkinson of Grimethorpe received the scroll on behalf of his son, 36-year-old Malcolm, who was killed when a Sea King helicopter in which he was travelling crashed into the sea. Barnsley MBC (BMBC, Mayoral Archive)

Mason with his agent Arthur Stokes and supporters, including Pauline Smith and Judith Watts, outside Barnsley Labour Party headquarters during the June 1983 General Election. (MA)

For many years a free film show for pensioners and people with disabilities was organised by Roy Mason at the Odeon cinema in Barnsley and much appreciated by all concerned. This festive occasion dates from 1985. (Roy Sabine)

Ian MacGregor (extreme right) being greeted with flour bombs at Brodsworth Main, picketing Bentley miners and their Scargill-imaged banner nearby, 2 February 1984. The Scot-American 'hatchet man' had been preferred to Mason as NCB chairman, succeeding Norman Siddall in September 1983. (BEC)

Pickets and their barricades near the railway bridge at Orgreave, 16 May 1984. (A Wakefield)

Enjoying a day out at Scarborough, organised by Mason for the children of striking miners during the 1984/85 dispute. (MA)

Prime Minister Margaret Thatcher looking understandably pensive as Roy Mason points to a montage of images he had assembled relating to the 1984/85 miners' strike under the theme Lest We Forget, part of the annual exhibition of artwork by MPs and peers, 2 July 1985. One of the images has a 'V' for Victory for the Miners superimposed over a photograph of Mrs Thatcher. (MA)

Back on the main line: setting off the City of York on the Barnsley to London direct rail (InterCity 125) service, the first for more than twenty years, 12 May 1986. (MA)

WE ARE UNEMPLOYED
WE ARE NOT PROBLEMS
WE DO HAVE RIGHTS
WE ARE IMPORTANT

Poor fall further behind

obless tot pproaches ecord leve

MPLOYMENT d an unexpected December and y to surge to a level in Jan- official figures yesterday.

nont se b ; or e. T ie io

100,000, which would push the unemployment total well above the previous peak of 3,346,000 recorded last September.

In Sheffield more than 600 more men claimed benefit last month

Mexborough, than 23,300 work, 22.3pc, November.

Doncaster Barnsley (18.8 hard hit with (14.4pc) and le nal

THE FIGURES IN FULL

AREA	TOTAL JOBLESS	CHANGE ON PREVIOUS	UNFILLED	CHANGE

Poverty in Barnsley: produced by Mason in 1986, this booklet highlights the 'increasing poverty over the past five years of Tory administration' which has 'shattered individuals, families, small communities and our local economy'. By the end of 1985, in the wake of the miners' strike, unemployment in the Barnsley Travel to Work Area had reached almost 19 per cent. It would take many years for recovery, in the wake of the miners' strike. (MA)

Roy and Marjorie Mason (extreme left) talk to HM the Queen during the royal visit to Barnsley, 12 December 1986. Councillor John ('Jack') Wood, the Mayor of Barnsley, can be seen making the introductions. After lunch at the Town Hall, Mayor Wood later said that the Queen was 'absolutely delighted' at seeing and meeting so many Barnsley people. (MA)

Three generations of the Mason family in 1986. Back row (left to right): Kevin and Jill Martin (daughter), Allen and Susan Duke (daughter); front row: Caroline, Lady Marjorie and baby Andrew, Lord Mason and Steven. (Stan Plus Two)

A shaft of light falls on Margaret Thatcher at the Dispatch Box during PM's questions in a packed Commons chamber during the Thatcher-Kinnock era. Roy Mason is now a backbencher, arrowed. Detail from a painting owned by Lord and Lady Mason by the well known portrait artist June Mendoza. (Mendoza/MA)

Part Nine

Peer of the Realm
1987-present

'It's the one forum in Britain where genuine, hands-on experience can make itself heard.'

The Armorial Bearings or 'Achievement' of Arms of The Rt Hon The Lord Mason of Barnsley, PC, D Univ, DL (MA/College of Arms)

Overview

Until a recent illness in 2008, Lord Mason has been a regular attender at the House of Lords, never missing a Session, a remarkable record of more than twenty years continuous service since his introduction to the Chamber. Accompanied by Lady Mason, this has often involved travel by a chauffeured security car (public transport being ruled out), and protection officers; and of course living in various 'safe houses' in London. Out of office, however, the accommodation was not grand, a flat above a police cell and Army barracks being used during periods of high alert; and then small hotels.

Attendance at Labour Party conferences involved a considerable amount of planning and logistics by the protection people of Special Branch. Mason recalled that this could include up to six rooms having to be booked so as to be able to accommodate everyone. Close guard was kept on himself in and outside of the conference headquarters.

During and since Northern Ireland the Masons have had to live and adapt to round the clock protection, reviewed by the Intelligence Services on a regular basis. As late as 1999, when I first visited Lord Mason when researching a local book, my appointment was booked in advance and my identity checked by two armed police officers who 'lived' in a hut attached to the Masons' Victorian house in Barnsley. Electronic devices were also evident and no doubt some discrete and CCTV cameras always operative.

From the early 1990s, protection at the Masons' home became much more evident and over the years numerous known events and incidents have reinforced this requirement. During an Old Bailey terrorist trial, for example, Mason's name appeared in a list of high profile targets used as evidence by the prosecution counsel. Shortly afterwards, in 1993, an IRA suspect arrested in Limerick was found with documents in his possession suggesting a surveillance operation on Mason. The material was so detailed that it included reference to his regular attendance at the Oakwell football ground, to support Barnsley. Sniffer dogs were subsequently used to check seating before every home game. Then, in 1994, a stray piece of paper found near the Masons' home contained a sketch of the area leading up to the house. The following year, a stranger, carrying a Kalashnikov rifle, was arrested within a short distance of the Masons' Yorkshire coast holiday cottage; and in 1995, what appeared to be bomb-making materials were found in a binocular case close to the Masons' home.

Going for a walk, traveling to a pub or restaurant, attending an official or social function, just meeting friends, even going on holiday or, as we have seen, watching Barnsley Football Club all had to be carefully vetted and protected. Twice, when Mason underwent a minor operations, a protection officer donned a surgeon's gown and stood next to Mason during the entire procedure.

No former Northern Ireland secretary has had such a high and continuous level of protection for such a long period, and for such high public cost, something that galled Mo Mowlam (Mowlam, 134) who complained that she had relatively little or no security after her own Ulster stint. When one of Mason's successors, Jim Prior, ignored protection at his London residence in 1992 an 'active service unit' bombed his flat.

But Mason's situation was different. Intelligence obviously confirmed time and time again that he continued to be at considerable risk, something that he had been very well aware of in the wake of the 'Stuff Mason' campaign and, because of his firmness in refusing to see Maze inmates as political prisoners or indeed allowing them any special status. In September 1993, Martin McGuinness, the former IRA member (and now deputy First Minister of Northern Ireland) was reported in *The Guardian* that Mason was the only Northern Ireland Secretary of State who had 'impressed' and 'beat the shit out of us'.

Innocent activity once resulted in a major security alert when a roof-top council worker carrying a rifle for shooting nuisance pigeons was spotted by the police on a building not far from Mason's home. Marksmen were deployed until it was fortunately realised that it was just a council cull.

On a lighter note, once when Mason was crossing the footbridge over Walton Hall lake, near Wakefield, one his officers accidentally dropped a gun, just short of it falling into the water;and on another occasion when the Masons were playing crown green bowls an officer's firearm spilled onto the grass, much to the great shock and surprise of hitherto sleepy onlookers.

The Right Honourable Roy Mason, having been created Baron Mason of Barnsley - as a life peer of the realm - was, in his ceremonial robes, introduced in the Lords' Chamber between the Lord Cledwyn of Penhros and the Lord Wilson of Rievaulx shortly after Prayers (2.30 pm) on 3 November 1987. The new Member soon adapted to the change of pace and indeed more civilised debating forum, making, as we shall see, many contributions, in both speeches and in writing.

Baron Mason's maiden speech took place only three weeks later, on 25 November 1987, when he intervened in a debate relating to the privatisation and impending privatisation of electricity and coal industries. After outlining his own early experience in mining, with both authority and wit - 'I worked there [underground at age 14] in a seam which was 1ft. 10 inches high. Even the the mice were bowlegged' - he went on to describe the 'severity of the recent run-down of the industry' and the high unemployment in his home town of Barnsley. 'To break it up [the coal mining industry] and sell it off to private speculators, is going back to the pre-vesting days of cut-throat competition with district against district, pit against pit and man against man,' he said. In response, and also with a touch of humour, Lord Marsh congratulated Mason for his speech and said that if he ever decided to campaign for the presidency of the National Union of Mineworkers 'he will receive enthusiastic, unqualified all-party support.'

Mason found the switch to the Second Chamber 'an unbelievable change', and was certainly not used to the 'utter civility, the serenity and courtesies of their Lordships' in which legislation is vetted and passed 'by your leave' or 'after you my Lord'. After a year, he still had no desk or telephone, reduced to 'wandering through their Lordships' House like a leaf on a breeze'. Mason was surprised at the overcrowding but was impressed by the legislative role of the Lords, Government, Opposition and Cross-Bench peers working hard and for many hours.

As a relatively young peer, coming fresh from the Commons with 34 years of parliamentary experience, including high offices of State, Mason was able to contribute with authority on a wide range of regional, national and international issues. On 9 December 1987, for example, he spoke in the debate about East-West Relations, expressing caution about Russia's 'aura of glasnost' and poor record of human rights, particularly in their treatment of 'refuseniks', Jews who have been refused leave. He also warned about not being taken in by the Soviet 'propaganda machine' which 'has never been so lubricated'.

Matters relating to the environment and opencast mining was the subject of a notable speech in the Lords on 13 January 1988, criticising the Government's failure to sign the protocol to the international convention on long-range transboundary air pollution. He also wanted to know why Britain had not joined other nations of Europe pledged to cut back sulphur emissions. During the same speech, mason was critical of the 'quick profit motive' of opencast coal mining and its adverse environmental impact. A month later, he spoke at some length in the Lords' Chamber to encourage the Government to enact an amended Clause 28, to provide that local government 'shall not intentionally promote homosexuality or homosexual activities'.

Interestingly, as early as 1992, Mason spoke about the considerable advantages to be gained from a national identity scheme, referring to the growing problems of illegal immigration, drug trafficking, criminals and suspected terrorists. He was in favour of the introduction of 'a mandatory, simple scheme' which would (in 'no-go' housing estates) 'help lift the veil of fear from many people'.

In November 1998, Mason paid tribute to his noble friend Lord Lofthouse and his long campaign for the recognition of emphysema as an industrial disease qualifying for compensation. But he expressed great concern about the length of time that many claimants and widows of claimants were having to wait for payments. Similarily, in December 2000, Mason contributed to an important debate, also initiated by Lord Lofthouse, on the same subject, asking the Minister for information on the number of payments, expedited claims, additional payments and number of deceased claimants.

The number and scope of Mason' speeches and questions tabled over a 20 year period has been considerable. Sampling Hansard, there are records of his contributions relating to angling, animal rights, Atlantic salmon, the beef industry, cancer (treatment and research), charges for sight tests, clean coal technology, Defence, the Energy White Paper, greenhouse gas emissions, health and safety, North Sea fishing, marine conservation, mentoring, motorways, museums, NATO, Northern Ireland, nuclear power, Objective 1 status, open spaces, pit closures, police surveillance cameras, Prevention of Terrorism Act (1989), Prince's Youth Business Trust, professional football, security at Westminster, shipbuilding, small businesses, smoking in public places, Training and Enterprise Councils, unemployment in Yorkshire & Humberside, weights and measures, and many others too.

Perhaps Mason's longest and hardest campaign, and one that he has been most pleased to be linked, relates to getting recognition for the survivors of the circa 48,000 Bevin Boys - named after Ernest Bevin, the wartime Minister of Labour and National Service - the 'forgotten conscripts', balloted and volunteered into the mines during the Second World War. Following a request for help from their Association, Lord Mason secured the support of the Admiral of the Fleet, Lord Lewin, whose ADC happened to have been a Bevin Boy. Despite many obstacles, approval was granted from Jack Straw for a contingency of the men to march by the Whitehall Cenotaph, wearing miners' helmets, starting at the annual Service of Remembrance, in 1998. In 2007, Lord Mason tabled a question to HM's Government, enquiring as to whether 'medals, ribbons or lapel badges' should be provided and awarded to Bevin Boys as a mark of war service recognition. A further campaign gained momentum (as did one on the behalf of Land Army women), Energy Minister Lord Truscott and Prime Minister Tony Blair informing an appreciative Commons in June 2007 that the first badges would be issued in 2008, on the 60th anniversary of the demobilisation of the last Bevin Boys, in 1948. The first badges were awarded by Prime Minister Gordon Brown at a Downing Street reception on 25 March 2008. Lady Mason received her Women's Land army badge on 23 July 2008.

Life in Pictures

The Rt. Hon. The Lord Mason of Barnsley PC

The significance of Lord Mason's Armorial Bearings or "Achievement" of Arms is as follows:-

The silver Roses denote his being a Yorkshireman, the Portcullis stands for Parliament and refers also to Lord Mason as a Parliamentarian who has held several Offices of State ~ Post Master General, Minister of Power, President of the Board of Trade, Secretary of State for Defence and Secretary of State for Northern Ireland. The embattled "fesse" or band with its red 'masonwork' alludes to Lord Mason's name and the particular skills of those to whom it was given in the past. The Beaver features also in the Arms of the London School of Economics, at which Lord Mason received his education. The crest of a demi-lion, which is placed upon a Baron's helmet, is a symbol of industrial energy fuelled by the getting of coal, to which the miners' pick-axe and lamp are references, the said lion holding aloft in its right paw a miner's pick-axe and resting its left paw upon a miner's lamp. The Escarbuncle of 14 rays alludes to Lord Mason's 14 years as a Miner. The Miner and the Glass Blower compare with the supporters granted in 1913 to Barnsley, whence Lord Mason derives his nomen dogmatist "Mason of Barnsley". The Industries of Coal and Glass being the backbone of Barnsley's economy during his 34 years as Member of Parliament for Barnsley. The motto "INTEGRITY AND COURAGE" states the characteristics with which Lord Mason of Barnsley has conducted his career.

Explanation of the Mason Armorial Bearings (College of Arms)

Mason was introduced into the House of Lords by his supporters, Baron Wilson (Harold, of Riveaux) and Baron Hughes (Cledwyn, of Penrhos). (MA)

Lord and Lady Mason at the House of Lords with cricket umpire Harold 'Dickie' Bird, who was celebrating his 100th international appearance, on 23 May 1988. Also presents are friends John and Pat Perry of the Livermead Cliff Hotel, Torquay. (MA)

A rare photograph of Mason alongside Lord and Lady Wilson (of Rievaulx) and Lord Callaghan (of Cardiff), c.1990. Wilson made few public appearances after Mason's introduction to the Lords, suffering increasingly from Alzheimer's disease. He died in 1995 and the Masons attended his memorial service. (MA)

A special image from Lord Mason's archive, a signed photograph, circa 1992, of six past and present Labour leaders. They are (left to right): Lord Callaghan, John Smith (then Leader), Lord (Cledwyn) Hughes (Opposition Leader in the Lords), Michael Foot, Lord (Harold) Wilson and Neil (now Lord) Kinnock. (MA)

Mike Atherton, England cricket captain, 1993-98, receives a Slazenger cricket bat from Lord Mason, c.1995. The world-famous sports goods manufacturer then functioned from its historic factory in Barnsley where tennis balls for Wimbledon were also made. (MA)

The Lords in Session during 1995. Lord Mason is seated on the second row of the Government benches, facing the Clerks, second left, next to Lord (Jack) Ashley (wearing neck brace). (MA)

In Barnsley, outside the Town Hall, with a small contingent from the Bevin Boys' Association (left to right): Harold Jackson, Phil Wood, Len Hirst and Warwick Taylor. (MA)

Proud to wear a Bevin Boy's helmet, in Mount Vernon Hospital, Barnsley, 25 April 2008. (BEC)

Mason enjoying a joke with Prime Minister Tony Blair at the peers' annual party, c.1999. Blair was often complimentary to Mason whenever they met, particularly regarding his stint as Secretary of State for Northern Ireland. (MA)

With armed police protection offices outside his Barnsley home in 1999. (BEC)

This adapted shed (a replacement of a more basic structure), attached to the Masons' house, for many years was used for the convenience of his police protection officers. The strategic placing of CCTV cameras also ensured that no visitor escaped scrutiny, day and night. (MA)

This photograph, taken by Lord Mason, won the right to be exhibited at the All Party Photography Group's annual exhibition, sponsored by Jessops, in 2003. It shows Prime Minister Tony Blair with Lord Callaghan at the unveiling of a bronze bust of Callaghan in the Speaker's House. Blair regarded Callaghan as a 'giant of the Labour movement'. (MA)

On the terrace at Westminster with grandson Steven and daughter Jill, July 2001. (MA)

Two old colleagues and friends: Lord Mason and Lord Callaghan at the ceremony described above. Callaghan was the longest living former British prime minister in history, dying on the eve of his 93rd birthday, in March 2005. (MA)

The Masons with Mo Mowlam, the much respected former Northern Ireland Secretary who oversaw the talks leading to the 1998 Good Friday agreement. Diagnosed with a brain tumour in 1997, she died aged 55, in 2005. In the mid 1980s, before Mo became an MP, she lived in Barnsley, working as a tutor at the Northern College of Adult Education. (MA)

The Masons with Lord and Lady Longford, c.2000. Lord Longford (7th Earl, Frank Pakenham), who died in 2001, was a ministerial colleague of Roy Mason during the Wilson administrations and had a great interest in Irish history (he also was an Irish peer). Longford is well remembered for his efforts to rehabilitate prisoners, and most notably for his campaign to release the Moors murderer, Myria Hyndley. (MA)

On the Scottish island of Iona, at the grave of John Smith, who served as Labour leader from July 1992 until his sudden death from a heart attack on 12 May 1994. (MA)

Lord and Lady Mason with an old friend, Baroness Falkender, who as Marcia Williams was private and then political secretary to prime minister Harold Wilson, taken in c.2001. Williams chose the title of Lady Falkender of West Haddon (in Northamptonshire) when she became a peer in 1974. (MA)

On the Woolsack, from 2006 the seat of the Lord Speaker (currently Baroness Hayman), but used by the Lord Chancellor when he welcomed Mason as a new peer to the Lords in 1987. Today, Baron Mason is one of over 600 life peers. (BEC)

In front of the Steps of Throne and Throne in the Lord's Chamber, 2007. The Throne is used by the Sovereign during the State Opening of Parliament. (BEC)

In part of the House of Lords Library, an essential support facility used by Members for research, reference and loans. Mason often made use of the Library and its staff for background or specific information on a wide variety of subjects. (BEC)

In the Lords lobby, with his great friend, Baron Lofthouse of Pontefract (Geoffrey Lofthouse), like Mason a former Yorkshire miner, 2007. Lofthouse was chosen as First Deputy Speaker in the Commons shortly after Betty Boothroyd took the Chair in 1992. For many years Geoffrey has fought to obtain compensation for mineworkers suffering from industrial disease. At his introduction to the Lords, in 1997, one of Geoff's two supporters or sponsors was Baron Mason. (BEC)

Detail from the painting in the background of the previous photograph, looking across from the Woolsack towards the Labour peers. Lord Mason is is on the second row from the front, fourth from the left aisle. (BEC)

Lord Mason at Westminster where he has worked continuously for 56 years, one of the longest parliamentary associations in modern times. (MA)

With Lady Wilson at the Labour Peers' party, July 2007. (MA)

On the terrace at the Houses of Parliament, with myself, my wife, Angela (right) and daughter, Hannah, June 2008. (BEC)

Part Ten

People, Passions and Presentations

'She [Lady Mason] has been a lady all her life.'

Lord and Lady Mason, a photograph specially commissioned for their 60th wedding anniversary, 2005. (Stan Plus Two of Barnsley)

Overview

Having entered the Lords, Mason was also able to make use of his new status and a little more time on voluntary work, charities, hobbies and interests. This final part of the book will hopefully give a small flavour of Lord and Lady Mason's very active life which continues to the present day.

Lady Mason continued to give time to support Lord Mason in many of his diverse activities and public engagements, as ever an unofficial secretary; and also was involved in work for charities such as the Yorkshire Cancer Trust. In 1987, in response to a local press interview, Mason remarked that if anyone should have been honoured for public service, it should be his wife, Marjorie, saying: 'My becoming a Lord won't make her a lady. She's been a lady all her life.'

At the beginning of 1987 Lord Mason agreed to be Chairman of the newly established South Yorkshire Area of The Prince's Youth Business Trust, an organisation dedicated to help disadvantaged and unemployed young people (aged 18-29) to establish their own businesses. He remained in office until 2001, retiring after fourteen years service. During this period the Trust had taken 2,200 unemployed young men off benefit and helped them set up in business, awarding grants and loans totalling almost £3 million. He presided over 162 board meetings covering the Trusts' activities in the Barnsley, Doncaster, Rotherham and Sheffield areas.

In 1987 Lord Mason also accepted the chairmanship of an even more local business organisation: the Barnsley Business Innovation Centre (BBIC). A private company (limited by guarantee), it was established to foster the development and growth of technological and knowledge-based enterprises; and in the process generate economic growth in the Borough of Barnsley. During Mason's involvement this public/private organisation has assisted over 220 businesses and expanded from one building and 15 business units to four buildings and 116 units. In 2001, for example, the electronics company Siemans opened an e-business information and advice centre at the BBIC, one of the first of its type in the UK. The BBIC's operation in the Barnsley area has therefore made a significant contribution to the local economy, creating high quality employment and enhancing economic development.

Public service continues to the present-day. In 2008 Lord Mason agreed to serve as President of the Experience Barnsley project, dedicated to establish a new interactive centre of heritage, research and learning within Barnsley's historic Town Hall.

The last 20 years or so has also included further honours and recognition in many fields. In 1993, Mason was awarded an Honorary Doctorate at the new University of Sheffield Hallam and as recently as 2005 he was presented with a Doctor of Civil Law degree by his old Cabinet colleague Lord Glenamara (formerly Ted Short), Chancellor of Northumbria University. Undoubtedly the greatest accolade came in November 2007 when he was given the Freedom of the Metropolitan Borough of Barnsley in a moving ceremony at Barnsley Town Hall.

Like Harold Wilson, Mason always enjoyed pipe smoking and whilst still an MP formed the Lords and Commons Pipe (and later cigar) Club, which had 73 members by 1996. As Covenor, he gathered members together on a variety of occasions or visits, even on Non-Smoking Day. He even designed a tie specially for members. The Club's symbolic tobacco jar, was commissioned by Mason from a piece of stone that once formed part of the Palace of Westminster before it suffered wartime bomb damage. In 2001, he described the high tax on tobacco as a 'smugglers' charter', encouraging the illegal import of cheap cigarettes which had a higher, and therefore more dangerous to health, tar content; and opposed the Government's plans for a ban on tobacco advertising, smokers being 'singled out for public and unfair chastisement'. When Baroness Blackstone dared to suggest that smoking should be banned from the peers' Writing room, Mason started a petition, eagerly signed by 30 angry lordships, including several non-smokers.

Angling has been a tremendous interest and activity for Mason since he was boy living near the Barnsley Canal. Typically, however, piscatorial pursuit has not just been a recreation, but a subject that he spoke knowledgeably about in both Commons and Lords - renown as the Anglers' Friend at Westminster; and one where he initiated improvements for disabled anglers. Well known as patron of the English Disabled Fly Fishers, and his association with the Handicapped Anglers' Trust and Anglers' Conservation Association, Mason regularly organised fund-raising team events, enlisting the active support and participation of parliamentary colleagues via the Lords and Commons Fly Fishing Club (which he founded), and a range of celebrities, including Bernard Cribbins, Geoffrey Palmer, Chis Tarrant, Roger Daltry, the late Chris Brasher, Eddie Gray and Jack Charlton. In 2007, the time had come for Mason to hang up his vast collection of tackle, giving them to Barnsley Trout Club, in order to encourage more youngsters to take part in a sport that has meant so much to him.

Another great passion is supporting Barnsley Football Club, something that Lord Mason has done since the age of 10, incredibly, more than 70 years ago. The Masons rarely miss a home game at the Oakwell Stadium. In conjunction with the Barnsley Chronicle and Oakwell Review, for many years Lord Mason ran an annual football competition, the winner presented with a cheque for £100 and the runner up receiving £50, awarded on a match day.

Philately or stamp collecting has been an abiding interest ever since Mason was Postmaster General in 1968. Over the years, he collected a series of first day covers, filling over 30 albums. In addition, he would regularly buy sets of each new issue at the Commons Post Office and affixes them to Royal Mail First Day Cover Stamps which he gets cancelled with Commons, Lords, and Buckingham Palace datestamps. The covers are then signed by relevant individuals whenever possible, either personally or via friends, contacts or correspondence. Mason's collection attracted the interest of the British Philatelic Bulletin's editor who traveled from London to view his albums in 2001.

Back in 1976 Mason was chosen as Tie Man of the Year. Always smart, he had attracted the attention of the fashion trade and the tie manufacturers in particular. The occasion boosted a lifelong interest in tie collecting and design (or cravatology) which had begun even earlier when he designed an MoD tie. Noticing that neither peers nor MPs had an identifiable neckwear, he began by creating a tie for Labour members. Others followed. Harold Wilson asked and got a Chequers tie, the bust of the Speaker George Thomas in Parliament has a Mason tie and he has created appropriate and symbolic versions for the Cabinet members of 1974 (two administrations in one year), NATO, NUM 1984/85 strike, RAF All-Party Group of MPs, Labour Whips, and a PLP charity tie, profits going to their Benevolent Fund. Commissions include a tie for the Police Federation and a tie for the disabled, even a protection officer's design, all in all over 26 carefully researched versions.

Mason's interest in Art is also well known. For many years he served as President of the Yorkshire Watercolour Society, attending numerous events and exhibitions. Having a good eye for paintings and drawings, in 1979 he discovered - hiding in a Barnsley 'junk shop' - a large lost portfolio of the work of Pearl Binder (1904-1990), completed 1929-35, which included notable coal mining lithographs. Binder subsequently married Lord Elwyn Jones, later Lord Chancellor. In the 1990s Mason commissioned a painting and set of limited edition prints to commemorate the breaking of the Berlin Wall. Created by his friend, the famous Yorkshire watercolour artist Ashley Jackson, the proceeds from the print sales were donated to the Romanian Orphan Appeal. Over the years, Mason has also collected an important portfolio of original political cartoons, featuring himself, each signed and presented to him by the originator.

Life in Pictures

Welcoming Prince Charles, the President and Founder of the Prince's Trust, Abbeydale Industrial Hamlet, Sheffield. (MA)

With Prince Charles at Mexborough Business Centre, 17 November 1993, Lord Mason (centre) representing the South Yorkshire Region of the Prince's Youth Business Trust. (MA)

The Board, staff and wives of the South Yorkshire Region of the The Prince's Trust join Lord Mason for a celebratory luncheon in honour of his long service, May 2001. (MA)

With Tim Milburn, Chief Executive of Barnsley Business and Innovation Centre. (MA)

Receiving one of the first Honorary Doctorates (D.Univ) awarded by the University of Sheffield Hallam University in 1993. (MA)

With Lord Glenamara, formerly Edward 'Ted' Short MP, who presented his old cabinet colleague Lord Mason with an honorary Doctor of Civil Law degree in June 2005. It was one of the last official duties of Glenamara who retired as Chancellor of Northumbria University shortly afterwards. Mason's citation includes reference to a 'legacy' which 'will continue to touch the lives of generations to come'. Glenamara (b.1912) is (in 2008) the oldest sitting Member of the House of Lords. (MA)

On Wednesday 21 November 2007 Lord Mason received a great honour when he was given the title of Honorary Freeman of the Metropolitan Borough of Barnsley at a special ceremony at the Town Hall. The citation refers to his 50 years as a trade unionist, parliamentarian, Minister of the Crown under two Prime Ministers, holding high offices of state, most notably for Defence, Northern Ireland, a Privy Councillor and Peer of the Realm. Councillors Stephen Houghton, Ronnie Fisher and Mike Stokes paid tribute to Lord Mason's lifetime achievements. In his acceptance speech, and with great emotion, Lord Mason spoke about the great love and support that he had received over the years from his wife, Marjorie. Here he is seen with the Mayor, Councillor Len Picken who was also a former mineworker. (BEC)

With Roger Daltry, Bernard Cribbins and friends, at a successful charity fly fishing competition. (MA)

Christening a Wheelyboat, for the use of disabled anglers at Walton Hall lake, near Wakefield. (MA)

Two massive rainbow trout caught by Mason from a stillwater lake. (MA)

With his angling pal, Chris Tarrant. (MA)

Mason presents a trophy to the famous Barnsley Blacks Team, angling world champion Dick Clegg (centre) looking on. (MA)

At Barnsley Football Club's Box Office, purchasing season tickets for the 2007/08 campaign. (Barnsley Chronicle)

Until very recently, Lord and Lady Mason occupied seats in the lower part of the East Stand of the Oakwell stadium, open to all the elements, rarely missing a game; and now (2008/09) look forward to watching The Reds via the disabled stand. (Barnsley Chronicle)

Barnsley supporters Stuart Bailey (left) and Samuel Allen receive cheques for £100 and £50 respectively, awarded by Lord Mason for his annual football competion, Oakwell Stadium, 2001. (MA)

Lord Mason with one of his special albums of First Day Covers. Those featured on the left are signed by Jimmy Savile; and the example on the facing page, commemorating the visit to Barnsley of HM Queen Elizabeth in 1986, is signed by Sir Nicholas Hewitt and Anthony Galvin of the Barnsley Chronicle. (MA)

Locally, Lord Mason has had a long association with members of the Barnsley Philatelists, providing and presenting a trophy in his name. Here he can be seen with their President, Ken Pemberton (right) and club members. (MA)

A party from the Lords and Commons Pipe and Cigar Club on a visit to the Falcon Pipe factory, London. Left to right are: Lord Broadbridge, Lord Hardy, Lord Mason, Lord Dixon, The Earl Grey, Lord Belhaven and Mr Stenton (manager). (MA)

Enjoying a smoke by the Club's stone pipe jar in the Lords' Library, before the public smoking ban came into force. (MA)

Campaigning for 'fair play' on tobacco taxation at Elstone's, Market Hill, Barnsley, in the late 1980s. (MA)

Mason as Tie Man of the Year in 1976. He is wearing a new tie with the town arms of Barnsley. It was this symbolic and meaningful aspect of the design that interested him, as talking points and for identity - a creative opportunity that he used with great success over many years. (MA)

Pointing to the 'Mason tie' on the bust of former Speaker George Thomas, the original consisting of a wig with a yellow daffodil placed inside, over the Mace, set on a green background to symbolise the green benches in the Commons Chamber. (MA)

Mason at the Cooper Art Gallery, Barnsley, at an exhibition of the Yorkshire Watercolour Society. One of the invited guests was his friend Betty Boothroyd, Speaker of the House of Commons. (MA)

Yorkshire Watercolour Society artist Bill Furness presents a portrait of Lord Mason to add to his collection, May 1996. (Barnsley Chronicle)

Lord and Lady Mason, his sister Edna (immediate left of Lady Mason) and friends, collecting for the Yorkshire Cancer Research at the ASDA supermarket in Barnsley, 2001. (MA)

Officially opening the restored Victorian midden at Cannon Hall, Cawthorne, near Barnsley, in September 1996. Lord Mason had spotted the two-seater set within a dilapidated structure several years earlier and initiated a renovation scheme, supported by Barnsley College and Barnsley Council. Left to right the party consists of Lord Mason, Lady Mason, The Mayor of Barnsley (Councillor C Wroe) and the Mayoress (Mrs Wroe), Ted Johnson (barnsley College) and Councillor Fred Clowery. (Barnsley Chronicle)

Lord Mason 'road tests' one of the wooden seats and reads his favourite weekly newspaper, when childhood memories of living at 'Long Row' came flooding back. (Barnsley Chronicle)

New Orleans in Barnsley? Mason performs on the drums in the Barnsley Jazz Band, with Stan Crowther (ex Rotherham MP) on guitar and Emmerdale's Seth (the actor, Stan Richards) looking over Crowther's shoulder. (MA)

The Masons with Stan Richards, after opening the country show and gala at Goathland, North Yorkshire, 1988. (MA)

Presenting a cheque courtesy of Darton Charity Gala to Crevesford Special School in Barnsley. (MA)

Laying the foundation stone at Barnsley Rugby Club's new headquarters, Shaw Lane sports ground, Barnsley, 29 January 2000. (Barnsley Chronicle)

A witty remark in the direction of his great friend, Dickie Bird at the latter's retirement dinner, Brooklands Restaurant, near Barnsley. (MA)

The Masons with another great friend, 'Percy Sugden', the Coronation Street actor Bill Waddington (1916-2000). (MA)

Time for a round of golf at the Hillies (9-hole) Golf Club, Wombwell, near Barnsley, 1997. (MA)

Lord and Lady Mason receive their first copy of the Spring 2007 Memories of Barnsley Magazine. (BEC)

Sources and Select Bibliography

I Original

The Mason Archive and Papers (private collection/Barnsley Local Studies & Archives/Cawthorne Village Museum)
We Cut The Coal (unpublished, collected papers, Mason Archive)
The Mason Cartoon Archive (private Collection of original cartoons and drawings)

II Books

Benn, Tony — (1) *Out of the Wilderness: Diaries 1963-67*, Hutchinson, 1987
Benn, Tony — (2) *Office Without Power: Diaries 1968-72*, Hutchinson, 1988
Benn, Tony — (3) *Against the Tide: Diaries, 1973-76*, Hutchinson, 1989
Benn, Tony — *Conflicts of Interest: Diaries, 1977-80*, Hutchinson, 1990
Benn, Tony — 4) *The End of an Era: Diaries 1980-90*, Arrow Books, 1994
Benn, Tony — *The Benn Diaries: New Single Volume Edition*, Arrow Books, 1996
Bird, Dickie — *My Autobiography*, Hodder & Stoughton, 1997
Brown, Colin — *Fighting Talk: The Biography of John Prescott*, Simon & Schuster, 1997
Callaghan, James — *Time & Chance*, Politico, 2006
Campbell, John — *Margaret Thatcher: The Grocer's Daughter*, Jonathan Cape, 2000
Campbell, John — *Margaret Thatcher: The Iron Lady*, Jonathan Cape, 2003
Castle, Barbara — *The Castle Diaries 1974-76*, Weidenfeld and Nicolson, 1980
Castleden, Rodney — *British History: A Chronological Dictionary of Dates*, Parragon, 1994
Cole, John — *As It Seemed To Me*, Weidenfeld & Nicolson, 1995
Crossman, Richard — *The Crossman Diaries*, Hamish Hamiliton & Jonathan Cape, 1979
Donoughue, Bernard — *Downing Street Dairy: With Harold Wilson in No.10*, Pimlico, 2006
Elliott, Brian — *Yorkshire Miners*, Sutton, 2004
Elliott, Brian — *Barnsley, 1890s-1990s*, Sutton, 1999
Elliott, Brian — *Pits and Pitmen of Barnsley*, Wharncliffe Books, 2001
Elliott, Brian — *Miners' Strike Day by Day*, Wharncliffe Books, 2002
Ellis, Walter — *The Beginning of the End: The Crippling Disadvantage of an Irish Childhood*, Mainstream Publishing, 2006

Hastings, Max & Jenkins, Simon — *The Battle for the Falklands*, Michael Joseph, 1983
Gormley, Joe — *Battered Cherub*, Hamish Hamilton, 1982
Langdon, Julia — *Mo Mowlam: The Biography*, Little, Brown & Company, 2000
Lawson, Nigel — *The View From No. 11*, Bantam Press, 1992
McGregor, Ian — *The Enemies Within: The Story of the Miners' Strike 1984- 5*, Collins, 1986

Marr, Andrew — *A History of Modern Britain*, Macmillan, 2007
Mason, Roy — *Paying the Price*, Robert Hale, 1999
Mercer, Derrik (ed) — *Chronicle of the 20th Century*, Longman, 1988
Mowlam, Mo — Momentum, Hodder & Stoughton, 2002
Pimlott, Ben — *Harold Wilson*, Harper Collins, 1992
Powell, Jonathan — *Great Hatred, Little Room: Making Peace in Northern Ireland*, The

Bodley Head, 2008

Ramsden, John (ed) *The Oxford Companion to Twentieth-Century British Politics*, Oxford, 2002

Robens, Lord *Ten Year Stint*, The Professional Library, 1972

Routledge, Paul *Scargill: The Unauthorized Biography*, Harper Collins, 1993

Scovell, Brian (ed) *Dickie: A Tribute to Umpire Harold Bird*, Partridge Press, 1996

Shelden, Michael *Orwell: The Authorised Biography*, William Heinemann, 1991

Taylor, Warwick *The Forgotten Transcript: A History of the Bevin Boys*, Pentland Press, 1995

The Times *The Times Guide to the House of Commons*, Editions of 1955, 1959, 1964, 1966, 1970, 1974, 1979, 1983, 1987, The Times

Westlake, Martin *Kinnock: The Biography*, Little, Brown & Company, 2001

Wheen, Francis *Tom Driberg: His Life and Indiscretions*, Chatto & Windus, 1992

III Magazines & Newspapers

Around Town Barnsley
Barnsley Chronicle
Belfast Telegraph
Daily Mail
Irish Times
Memories of Barnsley
News of the World
Sheffield Morning Telegraph
The Guardian
Hansard
The House Magazine
The Times
Yorkshire Post

IV Internet

www.bbc.co.uk/the oneshow (Bevin Boys)
www.number10.gov.uk (Prime Ministers)
www.barnsley.gov.uk (Barnsley MBC)
www.barnsley-chronicle.co.uk (Barnsley Chronicle)
www.cartoonmuseum.org (cartoons)
www.opal.kent.ac.uk/cartoon (cartoons)
www.news.bbc.co.uk (Northern Ireland)
www.archive.guardian.co.uk (Guardian Digital Archive)
www.parliament.uk (House of Commons & House of Lords)
www.wikipedia (on line encyclopedia)
www.news.bbc.co.uk/onthisday (On This Day)

Index